BATTLE AT WAR 1939-45

Edited by Adrian and Sarah Hall

ELSP

Published in 2019
and reprinted 2019 by
ELSP
in association with
Battle Museum of Local History

Origination by Ex Libris Press
www.ex-librisbooks.co.uk

ISBN 978-1-912020-73-7

CONTENTS

THE WAR IN THEIR OWN VOICES

INTRODUCTION

Published to mark the 80th anniversary of the outbreak of the Second World War, this account of Battle 1939-45 is intended to give a flavour of what life in the town was like then. There are also individual accounts by Battle people which give an idea of what happened in the larger theatre of war. Those whose world had previously been defined by living in a small East Sussex town, found themselves dealing with Dunkirk, bombing missions, escapes, the Long March from Poland, the Africa campaign, trouble in the Balkans, the siege of Monte Cassino and the forced repatriation of Russian POW's confirmed by Churchill, Roosevelt and Stalin at the Yalta Conference.

This book is based on new research from the recently discovered oral and written histories of those who experienced this traumatic episode in the history of the town. In that context, we record our thanks to those from the Battle community who helped, particularly the following: Simon Alexander, Linda Anonchans, Paula Batt, Battle Town Council, Peter Bridges, Brenda Clarke, Neil Clephane Cameron, Robert Catt, Clare and James Davidson, Gina and Kevin Doherty, Margaret and Robert Emeleus, Keith Foord, Joyce Gaudreau (*née* Adams), Corinne Gibbons, Alan Gillett, Mike Glazier, Pam Golding, Peter Greene, Keith Harmer, Hastings Library, Sam Hills, Michael and Wilma Hodge, Daryl Holter, Jill Johnson, Alan Judd, Peter Kemp, Sonia Kendall, George Kiloh, Raymond Lobb, Douglas Lowther, Simon Mansfield, Carol Milchem, Charlotte Moore, Richard Moore, Ian Norley, Ruth Pearson and family, Joanna Perkins, Colin and Pauline Raymond, Kevin Regan, Rother District Council, Alex Sabin, Howard Salmon, Peter Seymour, Ian and Mark Shore, Jim Spray, Anne and Trevor Wayne, Lucy and Ralfe Whistler. Any mistakes in conveying their advice and words to you in this book are ours alone.

For the benefit of younger readers, several of the personal accounts refer to pre-decimalisation weights. An ounce (abbreviated sometimes as oz) comprises just over 28 grams, 35 oz to the kilo. Three feet is just under a metre. Sometimes pre-decimalisation coinage is referred to: there were 240 pence (1d) to the pound, 12 to the shilling. 3d would be worth roughly 50p today.

We refer only in passing to some of the events which are well covered in other publications, such as the fatal bombing raid on Battle in February 1943. The story of Battle in the Second World War is not, even now, fully told: there will be further discoveries and stories coming to light. Creation of this book has involved the town's community, and brought many together, particularly those who remember the War. It will continue to be useful, we hope. If this book triggers memories, please contact bdhs66@yahoo.co.uk . The detailed basis of our research can be found in the chapter on Acknowledgements and Sources; and in the archive section of Battle and District Historical Society's (BDHS) website: www.battlehistory.btck.co.uk

Adrian and Sarah Hall
Battle, February 2019

BATTLE AT WAR

Battle before the war

What would it have been like in Battle just before and during the Second World War? At first glance, Battle High Street does not look very different now from how it did in the 1930s, with its historic buildings largely untouched. However, there are, of course significant differences.

In the 1930s, coming from the north, on the left you would have been greeted by the imposing Towers Hotel (now the site of the Fire Station) and on the right, a large cattle market (now Jempson's supermarket, other shops and the Library). Battle Abbey, although looking much like it does today, was then in private hands. Shops and facilities included seven hotels/pubs, six cafes/tearooms, four butchers, seven greengrocers/fruiterers, two ironmongers, five sweetshops/bakers, two shoe shops, a drapers, a blacksmith, four garages/motor agents, two cycle agents, a harness maker, boat maker, dairyman, corn merchant, coal merchant and an auctioneer who ran the cattle market, a cinema and a drill hall. There were two doctors, three dentists and two chemists. Long term residents of Battle would recognise the names of Tills the ironmonger, Thorpes the shoe shop, and Emeleus the chemist among others; Vicarys Garage and Sheppard & Son solicitors are just two of the names that are still found on the High Street. A major difference was the presence of the Newbery jam factory – during jam-making, the wonderful aromas could be smelt around Battle.

The roads of course were much quieter. There were motor cars but as early as 8th September 1939, strict petrol rationing was introduced, meaning that only officials and tradesmen could operate vehicles. So, cycles, horses, and pony traps were the way to get around – as well as walking of course!

Outbreak of war

The declaration of war on 3rd September 1939 did not come as a surprise. For over a year most people felt it was inevitable. The local cinema had screened several films with an aerial theme and there was fear that Hitler would use gas: the masks had been issued in 1938, along with Government handbooks distributed to all households, describing what would be regarded as essential civilian jobs to support the war effort.

Many Battle inhabitants heard the news of the declaration of war while in church – almost immediately, the air raid siren sounded and people rushed home. It turned out to be a false alarm on that occasion: it was rumoured that a British plane had been mistaken for a German one. Joyce Adams' memoir recalls that in her chapel they heard the air raid siren and then minutes later an air raid warden entered, going up to the Minister and whispering in his ear. The Minister announced that war had been declared with Germany. 'The congregation stayed until the all-clear sounded.'

How did life change?

The Second World War brought many changes to life in Battle:

Women: As conscription got underway, the numbers of men reduced and women took over many of their roles, for example in the shops. Not everyone approved of this but it gave women an unexpected chance to have a different life.

Evacuees: Right around the beginning of the war, on 3rd September 1939, children from London were evacuated to Battle and many other areas, among 1.5 million children removed from the metropolis, not counting 11,000 privately evacuated overseas, a practice to which Churchill put a stop. Houses were requisitioned where necessary. Reports suggest that the exercise was well organised and that the children were well looked after but as might be imagined there were some surprises due to social differences: one young evacuee from London's East End who had never been to the country, informed his host family that at home, he could not have left cabbages out at night as they would not be there in the morning. Another told his new family that if he had known how nice they would be, he would have brought his wristwatch! There were many consequences of this influx: unsuitable clothing, social mores, vermin, bedwetting and the financial burden on the receiving authorities, being among them. In Battle, so as to cope with the additional numbers, the school day was divided into morning and afternoon sessions, with local children going to one, the evacuees to the other. The local cinema also did its bit – evacuee children got in at half price, although it did not then take long for local children to start claiming they also were evacuees! However, the evacuees were soon moved to other areas of the country once it became clear that the East Sussex area was dangerous – as it turned out, it was part of 'bomb alley' and the planned route for a German invasion.

We found an account by a Battle boy – Cecil Bedwell, sadly now deceased – who on 21st July 1940 had to be evacuated to St Albans as he wanted to continue his schooling beyond the age of 14. It was too dangerous to carry on at Bexhill County Secondary School. He recalls vividly the hundreds of school children massed at Bexhill Station, and having to say goodbye to his beloved Meccano set. At St Albans the car driver took them round designated houses until finding someone in Oxford Avenue who would take Cecil in as well as his friend Brian. The house was cramped: the two owners, their child, the two Battle evacuees, another evacuee, and two adults who commuted into London. The living room had to be converted into a bedroom. Cecil next saw his parents in Battle for Christmas 1940 and after that a new host family had to be found for him, sharing a much larger house with eight others. "The father was Chief Valuation Officer for the London Borough of Holborn and was also deputy Civil Defence Controller so he resided at the Council offices and only returned home for a couple of nights about once a fortnight." The new host family made Cecil welcome but in his account, it is clear that his father worried about the higher social status of the host family, a common feature of the evacuations as different social groupings were mixed up. Cecil settled in, but there were safeguards. The headmaster at St Albans School appears to have acted *in loco parentis*, and during the summer holidays of 1941 the evacuee children had to check into school each day, writing periodic accounts of how they were getting on, so that evacuees not fitting in with their host families, could be moved. The school improvised to accommodate the evacuee children, with some odd outcomes, such as 'morning' assembly being at a quarter to four in the afternoon. Cecil says he was fortunate that from 1941 he could go home to Battle in the holidays – he had heard of some evacuated children who did not see their parents for four years. He returned to Battle for good in July 1942, having taken his School Certificate exam. He decided not to stay on in St Albans to take his Higher School Certificate because his father had been called up in 1941 and his Battle family needed him to be a breadwinner. He became a solicitor's clerk and lived in Battle all his life, at 4 Lower Lake.

Grafitti from the Royal Canadian Engineers,
Parks Yard, High Street by the Bull

Regiments**:** At first, the Devonshires came to Battle; these were followed by Canadian troops who were stationed in Battle Abbey, the Drill Hall (now replaced by the telephone exchange) and at an encampment near the Black Horse in Telham. The Canadian Corps was in charge of the defence of the Sussex coast between Fairlight and Hampshire for much of 1941 and into 1942. The townspeople made them welcome and invited them into their homes for meals; they were also popular with local children and at the dances. Looking at Britain as a whole, by 30 November 1946, 34,296 Canadian servicemen had married British brides. When a large number of the Canadians were killed in the raid on Dieppe, the loss was sorely felt: of 4,963 Canadians who embarked on that operation, 1946 became PoWs and 806 were killed, only 2211 returning to Britain. Towards the end of the war, the Somerset Regiment was stationed here.

Prisoners of war: In addition, as the war progressed, there were prisoners of war in the Battle area. According to local recollection, Italian PoWs were at Robertsbridge, in Bishop's Lane, for a short time, even though this camp is not officially listed. They were not held under high security and worked in the area, which would explain why even today it is remembered that at least one local child had an Italian father. There were also up to 552 German prisoners in a camp at Normanhurst in Catsfield. They were not allowed out until the war was over, except on particular occasions for example carol concerts at Christmas and to play football against the local team. According to a 1948 report, efforts to re-educate the German prisoners about what had happened and about the principles of democracy, had not gone smoothly. A factor may have been that many prisoners objected to the conditions at Mountfield Gypsum works where they were put to work. German pilots who crash-landed were treated fairly. If injured they were seen by Dr Eardley Davidson of the Martins Oak practice, before being handed over to the authorities. Robert Emeleus remembers seeing, at the end of the War, "a long column of PoWs marching up the High Street towards Normanhurst Court."

Raymond Lobb remembers that as a young boy he opened the front door of the farmhouse in Catsfield to find a German pilot standing in front of him. "There's a German here for breakfast" he said to his incredulous mother. On another occasion his father arrested a German pilot who got his Luger out – and handed it over. He was escorted direct to Normanhurst PoW camp.

***Local industry*:** Many local businesses were put on 'war work'. Senlac Metal Casements Ltd in Station Yard were, among other things, making ships' hatches, rifled rocket tubes, and mortar bomb fins. Howard Bros joinery works were engaged in making and repairing ammunition boxes, and also, because timber was in short supply, the conversion of timber recovered from damaged buildings, into plasterers' laths and tile battens, which were needed to make these buildings habitable once more. Jenner and Matthews, the light engineering firm, manufactured shell caps. Small workshops in Battle worked round the clock. These establishments would have worked a daily shift of 8 am to 7 pm. Vicarys garage was also involved.

Vicarys garage circa 1942 , L to R: Jeff Parkes, Lionel "Curly"Eldridge, John Luck, George Steel, Leon Gere, Tom Bowers, Fred Box

The wartime owner of Vicarys, Mr H G Seymour says: "I was informed early on that Army units were coming to Battle and that my workshops were to be used in the war effort and in particular I was to arrange for and train some of the men in these units in the rudiments of motor engineering, therefore it was essential that I stayed in Battle." Mr Seymour was also Transport Officer for the Civil Defence.

Pets and animals: At the outbreak of war some 750,000 pets across Britain were put to sleep arising from Government warnings about potential risks to their welfare. An organisation called NARPAC (National Air Raid Precautions Animals Committee) was created and very likely had a branch in Battle. Its job was to alleviate animal suffering due to wartime conditions; organise first aid posts for animals; and arrange emergency standings for horses and shelters for dogs.

Women's Land Army Women aged 18-25 not already in the Armed Services had to join the Women's Land Army or register with the Ministry of Labour which would allocate them jobs, often in a different part of the country. Women substituting for men in High Street shops caused adverse comment among some customers at the time. By 1943, 53% of workers were women. Throughout the war, Land Army women were helping on local farms and 'Lumber Jills' visited to cut down trees.

Food rationing began on 8 January 1940 and did not finish until 1954. Shortages arose from interruption to supply ships and certain foods all but disappeared, such as bananas. In August 1940, a ban was imposed on icing for wedding cakes: some people got round this by making cardboard covers decorated with crepe paper and flowers. New foods appeared such as spam (reconstituted meat) and powdered egg. Ration books were issued specifying *weekly* food allowances. For example, you were allowed four ounces (just over 100 grams) of meat or bacon: that's about the size of the palm of your hand, considered a healthy *daily* portion today. Other allowances were: two ounces of butter, four ounces of margarine, four ounces of cooking fat, two ounces of cheese and eight ounces of sugar. Fish was not rationed but was scarce and not always fresh; stews were made with offal, which likewise was not rationed. Vegetarian substitutes for meat were promoted like Lord Woolton pie, made from potatoes, swede, cauliflower and spring onions. Battle Parish Magazine in August 1940 promoted cauliflower cheese.

People were encouraged to 'dig for victory' and most people in the area had enough land to grow food – public allotments were undersubscribed but were quickly cultivated. Rosemary Bishop wrote for the East Sussex Women' Institute that children at Battle and Langton School tended the School garden, collected wool from hedgerows and acorns to feed the pigs and rosehips for a nutritious syrup. Those who remember these years never mention being hungry – certain foods may have disappeared but there were substitutes.

Alfred Lee outside his High Street butchers, VE Day 1945

Fred Holland, a Battle butcher, together with another butcher used to organise the local meat ration. Each morning they would go to the Hastings abattoir to pick up the allocated meat from government officials and distributed it to 24 other butchers across East Sussex, being careful to pick the best cuts for Battle customers of course! This service was suitably bureaucratised, with a government clerk to keep a record of the accounts. He remembers meat being very short, on some occasions only 10 old pence worth of corned beef per family per week, roughly £2 today. Locals however would keep rabbits and maybe a pig to help supplement their food. Foraging, especially by children, was standard: berries in season, crab apples, rabbits and so on; "See what you can find for tea", Raymond Lobb's mother used to tell him. Even conkers were collected because they had a wartime use, given the difficulty of overseas supplies: they contain starch, used for making acetone, an ingredient of cordite, a propellant for small arms ammunition and artillery.

Agriculture: The impact on farming was immense, not only in the replacement of farm hands by Land Army women who may or may not have had any previous experience of farming. Agriculture was closely regulated through committees – the East Sussex County War Agricultural Committee, based in Lewes, was in charge of the local area. Such committees had powers under the 1939 Emergency Powers (Defence) Legislation: if farmers did not obey their instructions, they had the power to remove farmers from their land without compensation or alternative accommodation [across the country, hundreds of farms were removed in this way although no local examples have come to light].

The difficulties faced by farmers were detailed in the records of Horsmans Farm in Sedlescombe. Gerald Gay, the farmer, expressed his frustration at a compulsory inspection of his farm as part of a campaign against rat infestation, in spite of the fact that as a fruit farmer he had no animals. More seriously, he suffered from the Government regulation of soft fruit prices: in 1941 and presumably other years, a table broke down prices into type of fruit, size of container and weight range. In a letter to the local National Farmers' Union, he protests at the 'ruinous price' which meant he was not able to recover a recent 2d increase in wages and would thus be selling at a loss. In the case of tomatoes, the maximum price schedule was even more detailed, with different prices for different times of the season and for different counties.

Towards the end of 1941, The East Sussex War Agricultural Committee issued a circular requiring new arable areas to be created in 1942; land that was to lie fallow must be sown with grass to enrich it with nutrients for its later return to arable.

Other difficulties included obtaining supplies such as containers. In 1942, Gerald was informed that military training by the Canadian Corps would be taking place on his land, but there was no mention of compensation for any damage to crops. A neighbouring farmer also complained about lack of help – on the one hand he thought Land Girls expected to be 'housed like the Ritz' but on the other hand his Land Army girl had left and he could not get a replacement, resulting in his son being overworked. As a result of that, land work was at a standstill and crops were spoiling. This cannot have been the only such occurrence.

Gerald Gay's farm must have also have undergone at least a couple of attacks from the Luftwaffe – in July 1942, he received an insurer's letter saying his damage claim could not be accepted because any enemy action prior to 17th April 1941 was not eligible for insurance cover. The second attack mentioned must have occurred later in 1941 as the company seemed to be willing to cover this instance. Judging from the letters, German aircraft had dropped about 19 incendiaries and an 'oil bomb' on the farm – oil bombs were drums between 10-120 kg in weight filled with oil and phosphorus, designed to set fire to crops on impact. The raid destroyed his strawberries, apple trees had to be uprooted to get at the remains of the bomb and, to cap it all, he alleged that the bomb disposal squad stole the picked apples!

At least one local farmer took his opportunities during the war: he rescued a crashed German pilot and discovered he was a dairyman by trade, so got him to help with the morning's milking before taking him to the police!

Defending Battle

Along with cities and towns across the country, Battle was quick to get volunteers organised to help with civil defence, a full list of helpers and organisers appearing as early as the 6th October 1939 census. An Emergency Committee was formed to co-ordinate activities; leading citizens were key to get the organisation underway. Volunteers would of course be expected to do civil defence volunteer jobs in the evening and their day jobs the following morning. As the war went on, tiredness became a significant problem.

Civil Defence

The District Organiser for Civil Defence (also known as the Air Raid Precautions – ARP) was Colonel W E Hume Spry, responsible for an area covering 188 square miles and 33 civil parishes. He was described as 'courteous, kind but very determined'. As early as 1936, he was insisting that Government precautions in the area did not go far enough in providing First Aid and Decontamination Centres; in 1939, he protested at cuts to personnel and equipment. The office and stores were in Old Brewery Building behind the High Street; there were four look-out posts, including one at Caldbec House on the top of the hill.

The centre of operations was at the Council Offices in Watch Oak at the north of the town and was protected by corrugated iron on the ceiling and shored up with substantial timbers, as well as sandbags. One warden remarked how being surrounded by old records and volumes, gave the office a 'medieval air'. There was also a large blast protector which made it rather dark, as well as wire netting over the windows. In the early days of the war, most of the volunteers slept there every night. They were trained in First Aid and in many other rescue skills – but in the early days, things were quiet. Later in the war, relief schemes were introduced so volunteers only went on duty every other night but at other times they still remained on call. Morale among the Battle ARP was maintained by a quarterly humorous magazine called 'Tin Hat'. The efficiency of the Wardens reporting in quickly was vital and so the following verse called 'Speed' was used to remind everyone:

"If you're doubtful what to do
Get that message to HQ
When you're sure you've done your best
Leave Control to do the rest."

Battle had one of the mobile rescue and casualty services and also was the regional headquarters for the Decontamination Service. There were 49 first aid points in the area and 350 volunteers, as well as 80 volunteers in the Auxiliary Fire Service. In addition, there were two volunteer Rescue and Demolition parties in the district. Each party had a lorry and full-time paid driver along with lifting equipment and covered a wide area – duties included making bombed houses safe, shoring up walls and removing fallen timber, before the search for survivors could begin. They turned off the electricity and water while the Gas Board turned off the gas. Then the search would begin for survivors, starting in the cellar if there was no-one under the stairs. A 'heavy rescue team' would then make the ruins safe for the longer term and clear away the rubble. Robert Emeleus remembers his mother Marjorie being lowered from a first floor window on a stretcher as part of a rescue exercise in Burwash. Fire Watchers became an additional part of civil defence as the number of incendiary bombs increased.

The Civil Defence were also responsible for training people to use gas masks – for example at the Watch Oak, there was a room which was filled with gas and you had to take off the mask and put it back on as quickly as you could before leaving. Doggerel verse was used to encourage local precautions:

"What a smell of musty hay
Get your gas mask right away
Put it on, don't look about
Phosgene's there without a doubt"

Home Guard: 'Dad's Army' as they came to be known started life as the Local Defence Volunteers but were renamed the Home Guard by Churchill himself. Nearly two million men had volunteered by the end of 1940. The original idea was that the Home Guard would operate locally to prevent small invasion forces from landing unobserved and make it hard for the invaders to reach the assembly points before the professional army arrived. They were also to guard tactical points and places of industrial importance. There was an active unit in Battle, one of whose duties was to guard road blocks, of which more later.

Some of Battle Home Guard: back row Warrant Officer Bill Catt left, Sgt Charlie Longley right
Front row left to right: Lt Quartermaster Allen; Capt Harry Judd; Co Commander Major Percy Woodhams; Medical Officer Capt Eardley Davidson.

While on the subject of the Home Guard, Simon Mansfield's father – a telephone engineer in Ticehurst during the war – left Simon the following story. "In September 1941, the Ticehurst Home Guard were on manoeuvres in the Staplecross/Cripps Corner Road area, with the local pub the White Hart as their target (this was the main defensive HQ for the area). After disembarking from Warrens Coach depot, in a wooded area, they marched south and eventually crept through the hedges and ditches up to the road in front of the pub. Here they let off a volley of blanks at the army defenders – much to their surprise – as the operation was supposed to have finished an hour earlier! The story ends on a high note as the publican opened the bar to allow the gallant Home Guard to quench their thirst."

Battle Army Cadet Force The Battle Army Cadet Force, shown in the labelled photo, was run by Lieutenant Jock Purvis, hairdresser; and by Sergeant Lou Sunnyside who worked at the flour mill. It met at the Drill Hall with a snooker table upstairs, a good place to meet socially. Stan Elliott (who bequeathed his archive to Battle Museum in 2014) said they were equipped with modern rifles, Sten guns and a Bren gun. There was a 25 yard rifle range at the rear of the Drill Hall for the smaller weapons while the larger ones were practised at a rifle range in Powdermill Lane.

Stan Elliott recalls an incident when Jock Purvis demonstrated to new recruits the importance of care in picking up a rifle to ensure it is not loaded. But he squeezed the trigger of the Winchester rifle he was holding and a bullet went through the roof. "That's the way NOT to do it" Jock quipped. The Cadets also had acquired a First World War Hotchkiss machine gun in working order along with ammunition of the time which Jock, a little headstrong, wanted to try out. His men dumped the ammunition in a pond while Jock was at the bar during the Drill Hall dance.

'Secret Army'/Special Patrols There were also small groups of men who were charged with the task of setting up a secret hideaway with about two weeks supplies to which they could go in the case of invasion. The idea was that they would form a resistance and carry out sabotage, designed to delay the invading forces – the rations were for two weeks only as that was as long as they were expected to survive. There were two such units known around Battle, one in Ashburnham and one in Telham. There is a

Battle Army Cadet Force 1945
***Back row** L to R: WO Joe Blackshaw; Cpl Baker; x; Pte Dennis French; L/Cpl Gerald Blackman; L/Cpl Mike Heasman; Pte John Christian; Pte Charley Bowers; Cpl Weller.*
***Centre row**: L to R: L/Cpl Derek Wood; Cpl Doug Lowther; Sgt Oliver; Capt "Jock" Purvis; Sgt Harold Thompsett; Sgt Young; Cpl Stan Elliott.*
***Front row:** L to R: Ron Haffenden; Larkin; Dave Marriott; Charley Carter; Hugh Soan; Dave Blackmore; Chapman; Cecil Power.*

rumour that the Canadians dug a network of underground chambers and tunnels under the house at Beauport Park, to be used as a hiding place for a resistance group should England be invaded. In fact the origin of this may be the Special Patrol's underground hideout, which was located in Ring Wood, west of Beauport Park Golf Course. On one occasion, led by Battle man Harry Thompsett, a gamekeeper, the Telham Patrol carried out an exercise to test their skills and those of the Canadian troops who were stationed in Battle Abbey. They managed to overcome the Canadian sentries and take the Commanding Officer captive. The Canadians naturally were a bit put out – wrongly assuming their attackers were the Battle Home Guard, a number of Canadian troops went to the Chequers Pub and beat up the wrong people in revenge!

Women's Voluntary Service The WVS was formed in 1938 by the Dowager Marchioness of Reading at the request of Sir Samuel Hoare, then Home Secretary. The Battle branch ran the 'Lord Leconfield canteen' from Old Church House in Upper Lake from 1941 – in six months, they served over 53,000 cups of tea and 1856 cakes! Tea, buns and scrambled eggs (from powdered eggs) were the usual offering. In winter, they served 100 hot suppers each evening. They also dealt with evacuation problems; acted as telephonists; provided transport; staffed a clothing depot which collected salvage including aluminium; ran sick bays and hostels; and even organised knitting parties. They also organised concerts for troops in Battle's Senlac cinema (now Burstow and Hewett).

WVS mobile canteen. Far left Mrs Stanley, then probably Mrs Sunnyside, unknown; far right Miss Buck

TocH, a Christian service organisation, ran a canteen above Starrs, (Costa today) and on Christmas Day 1940 gave a party at the Drill Hall for troops, including a 70lb Christmas cake. Local entrepreneurs made a living selling what today would be called "street food", for example Kath Emerick at Station Road, selling 'meat pies at 3d' each, roughly 50p today.

Kath Emerick: Street food

Royal Observer Corps Once enemy aircraft had appeared, the Royal Observer Corps provided an effective means of tracking their position. From July to October 1940, the Corps was at full stretch operating 24 hours a day, 7 days a week, plotting enemy aircraft and passing essential information to RAF Command Groups and Sector Controls. There were two roles: Class A undertook 56 hours duty a week, Class B up to 24 hours a week. They were the cornerstone of Air Marshal Hugh Dowding's air defence system, providing vital information during the Blitz campaign, enabling timely air-raid warnings and saving many lives. As a result of their role in the Battle of Britain, the Observer Corps was granted the title

Royal by King George VI and it became a uniformed Civil Defence organisation administered by RAF Fighter Command.

Local man Simon Alexander recalls that when his father Harry bought Le Rette farm in 1942, he joined the ROC and was based at the observation post at Sedlescombe. On one occasion, the German bombers were jettisoning their bombs very close to the farm and his father dsahed home to check everyone was safe – despite nine bombs falling close by, no damage was done.

Harry Alexander circa 1942 departs Le Rette for ROC duty, Nick Alexander in the foreground

Other anti-invasion preparations In 1940 the then Sir Alan Brooke was GOC Southern Command – later to become Chief of the Imperial General Staff. He was responsible for resisting the German invasion plan Seelowe (Sealion), issued in Hitler's Directive 16 on 1st August 1940. German Divisions would have attacked this part of East Sussex at Camber Sands, Rye, Winchelsea Beach, Bexhill and Pevensey. The German plan required the Surrey hills – represented by a line called "first objective" from Portsmouth through Petersfield, Guildford, Biggin Hill and Gravesend – to be reached within ten days. South of that line was the "covering" line for supplies, from Arundel through Mayfield and Ashford to Canterbury. The dropping zone for parachutists would have been east of Hythe. Plans for 'Operation Sea Lion' included the 99th Mountain Regiment landing at Winchelsea and heading straight for Battle, the objective being to secure the high ground south west of Robertsbridge which would serve first to achieve safe landing of succeeding waves, second as a springboard for the attack on London.

From 1941 onwards, Alanbrooke and other top commanders thought an invasion less likely. Heavy air raids on the night of the 6th seemed the start of the invasionand at 08.07 hours on the morning of the 7th the codeword "Cromwell" was issued to forces to stand by for action.

An invasion didn't come but the all-out attack on airfields continued until the 15th by which time the position in Kent was precarious. Hitler switched tactics to the bombing of London and other cities and on the 17th postponed the invasion. In 1941 British commanders concluded that a German invasion was too risky to be feasible. Nevertheless the threat of invasion was taken seriously until 1942 and the Home Guard remained on high alert.

Due to Battle's proximity to the south coast, it was part of a 20 mile high-security zone: to leave the area, you needed a permit; if visiting, your ID was checked by police at Battle station and you needed to explain the purpose of your visit. It was known as a 'fortress town'. At the coast, beaches were off limits with barbed wire and anti- aircraft guns, for example at Hastings.

Hastings front in 1944

Concealed pillbox at Pevensey Castle

There were anti-aircraft batteries in a number of places although no sign of them remains. But a pillbox embedded in Pevensey Castle is still visible today. Among the most obvious defence features you would notice were the extensive range of tank traps or 'dragons' teeth', which were designed to delay progress of tanks in the case of invasion. There were also two bren gun emplacements in the North Trade Road recreation ground – bren guns were considered a key part of anti-tank warfare because their fire would cause enemy tank crews to 'button up', limiting their field of vision and dispersing opposing infantry. How effective they would have been is hard to say but the imperative for them is confirmed in German sources.

The tank traps were large concrete blocks with as much buried underground as above. They were installed round Battle Abbey, St Mary's Church and across the field, as well as surrounding Wellington Gardens and the Watch Oak (pictured) , which served as a centre for local defence. Occasionally, the builders left their mark in the wet concrete, apparently some in Battle showed the RAF days' scores in the Battle of Britain! A few of these traps can still be seen in Battle, principally along the pathway to the nursery school by St Mary's Church; and there's one in a front garden in Saxonwood Road.

Removal and disposal of them at the end of the war was extremely difficult, apparently traction engines had to be deployed, and pneumatic drills to break them up. Some land owners just dumped them in remote areas, such as the 'tank trap graveyard' which still exists at Stephen's Crouch near Ashburnham.

In addition to the traps and to prevent enemy aircraft landing, farmers would leave sundry scrap vehicles and old tractors in the fields or areas of land and poles were sunk into the ground. As time went on, grass and weeds grew up through and about these obstructions and made them look very permanent.

Tank traps in Wellington Gardens

A tank trap in Susan Burton's Saxonwood Road front garden

There were also road blocks. Local man Stan Elliott remembered that the military set up tank barriers outside what used to be Pike House in Upper Lake (near the roundabout at the south of the town). There was just enough space between the two for a vehicle to be driven through, and the barrier could be closed by sliding a heavy section of rolled steel beams through one block and into the one on the other side. One Sunday morning, the Home Guard mounted an exercise to test this roadblock as a defensive position. They had some slit trenches along the top of Lake Field, which were manned by the defenders, who had a good view down Lower Lake towards the station. The 'enemy tank' when it finally appeared was actually a car which had been clad in sheets of corrugated iron being towed by another car. As it rounded the corner by the Chequers Pub it was attacked by the Home Guard, throwing home-made phosphorus bombs, seemingly with some success. However, the ever-present crowd of schoolboy sightseers had a grandstand view in the shaded recess between the pub and Lake House. It was not until they walked home that they discovered their clothes were smouldering, as phosphorus got to work in the heat of the sunshine.

Last, but not least of course, there were air-raid shelters. Each household was meant to construct one and there were also public shelters in Senlac Gardens and adjacent to Battle Abbey. Stan Elliott remembered that even children became involved in preparations. In September 1939, they were asked to bring spades and shovels so that holes could be dug in fields adjacent to the school in Marley Lane, to accommodate a number of Anderson Shelters, which were delivered in sections, complete with nuts and bolts and plans of how to construct them. Unsurprisingly, the school children were not strong enough, so their fathers helped get them built! Alongside the North Trade Road Recreation Ground, a trench was dug to allow people to jump in and take shelter if caught in the open air and there were no doubt others.

Battle people took all this with sardonic good humour. At the declaration of war, the Moore family gardener came into the kitchen with the news, where his wife was making breakfast. "The church bells are ringing- the

Germans are invading", he exclaimed. "There'll be no breakfast for them, then" replies the wife.

The blackout According to the *Hastings & St Leonards Observer* April 1944, the blackout times were 9.15 pm to 6.46 am, adjusted for changing daylight hours. During this period lights of any kind outside were not permitted and internal lights were only allowed if the window blinds obscured all trace of the light.

In her account of the war, Nella Last says that the first blackouts from 1st September 1939 meant that all street lights were extinguished, no car headlights were allowed, and windows were shuttered or curtained with heavy black material or paper. Later, torches and car headlights were allowed but masked to provide only a slit of light.

Joyce Adams in her memoir remembers that Pal Waite was the Battle lamplighter: "he would carry a long heavy pole which he would insert in the lamp and ignite the gas mantle." But the blackout rules meant no street lamps could be lit. Joyce says he resumed work after the war. The photo below of H G Seymour with son Peter working on a car at Vicarys, illustrates the practice of having a white stripe on the mudguards to help make cars more visible in the darkness.

White stripe mudguards to help in the blackout

Battle of course was on the route to London for German planes. On Saturday 7 September 1940, the Chiefs of Staff thought invasion imminent as a thousand German bombers came over the Channel: this was the opening salvo in the Blitz on London. Reports of sightings in Battle became more frequent. By 1941, a typical report from Mrs Whistler's No 4 lookout was, for 12th January, 'A good many planes over. Very heavy passage of planes backwards and forwards. Very heavy London barrage. Tremendous explosion in the direction of Northiam. Several bombs towards Brightling. Bomb and fire towards Catsfield. Heavy machine gunfire followed by flaming onions going upwards and tracer bullets coming downwards in the direction of Hastings'. Joan Holland recalled bombs coming down among her family's milking cows – by the time she arrived the village butcher was coming away and warned her not to go up there: it was a terrible mess, he had just been there with his humane killer. She reported that they received compensation for their lost livestock, but nowhere near what they were worth.

Much of the bombing in Battle was due to the German bombers jettisoning any leftover bombs before returning to the Continent. Simon Alexander, whose father owned Le Rette Farm, recalls one night when nine bombs were dropped around the house and buildings but was told by his father that the wires were crossed and so they only made moderate-sized craters. Clare Davidson, daughter of Dr Eardley Davidson, was delivered by her father on 30th May 1943 in a bedroom at Martins Oak, in the middle of an air raid!

The reality of the large number of high explosive bombs dropped in the Battle area, is brought home by Raymond Lobb's account. He recalls one going off behind what is today Littlewoods, near the Squirrel pub on the North Trade Road, making a hole about an acre in area and 40 feet deep. It was then filled, he says, with the unwanted debris of war: jeeps, cars, aircraft parts and so on. He recalls a heap of disarmed bombs being kept temporarily at the side of Powdermill Lane.

Most feared were the doodlebugs, which appeared later in the war: of the 8,000 of them that reached England, just over 2,000 fell in Sussex. They approached with a sound like a fiery motor cycle engine, then went silent. There were so many of them that there were rarely any air raid alarms. Rosemary Bishop reported that at school, "the older boys were trained to be spotters. This was usually for a two hour stint outside the school and sometimes the spotter wore a yellow badge. If a doodlebug was seen, they had to blow a whistle hard. We would dive for shelter under our desks. On one occasion one was seen approaching the School but the poor spotter was dumbstruck. However, we soon heard the familiar sound and dived for shelter. Fortunately, a Spitfire tipped the 'bug' and it veered award and fell in the sewage pit. The School was shattered with glass and plaster but nobody was hurt." The 'tipping' of the doodlebug was the main defence – if the bomb was going towards population or a facility, a pilot would fly beneath the bug and try and 'tip' its wing with the wing of his plane, with the aim of altering the direction of the bomb. This was of course incredibly dangerous and did not always work as intended: more than one resident reported thinking themselves safe with the bomb going past them, only for the wing to be tipped, and for it to turn back in their direction! Raymond Lobb recalls an RAF pilot over Catsfield tipping one doodlebug only to run into the path of another. The horror, as a young boy, of finding the pilot's body has stayed with him to this day.

On 2 February 1943, there was a raid by three planes on Battle, dropping three bombs: one skidded through the gatehouse into Battle Abbey and failed to explode – very fortunately, as the Canadian troops were storing two tons of gelignite in the Gatehouse; another landed in the cricket pitch, behind the George Hotel; and another killed Tom and Gladys Giles of Tickners at 75 High Street (now Martin's the newsagents). Why did the raid take place? Possibly, it was one of the 'Baedeker Raids', which targeted national monuments with the aim of lowering morale; maybe, they were targeting Newbery's Jam Factory (thinking it was something else) or the Senlac Factory.

So at least on that day, for all the tragedy of two lives being lost, Battle avoided a devastating explosion at the Abbey Gatehouse. Even so it would probably not have compared with the one in Tutbury in Staffordshire on 27th November 1944, probably one of the largest man-made explosions in history before the nuclear era. This was the site of an underground munitions dump deep beneath Upper Castle Hayes Farm. It is thought that in trying to remove the detonator from a 4000 lb bomb, an inexperienced airman used a brass hammer instead of a wooden one, the impact on his chisel causing a spark. The resulting explosion lifted 2 million tons of rock and soil thousands of feet into the air, vaporising the farm and all its inhabitants, human and animal. Widespread devastation was caused, a thick carpet of dust covered the area for miles, and 70 people were killed. A nearby dam was demolished, releasing 6m gallons of water. The explosion left a 12 acre crater 300 yards long, 230 yards wide, and 380 feet deep.

There were also two serious air crashes. The first involved a Wellington bomber which had been damaged on a raid in Boulogne – four of the Polish crew died, remembered at a public memorial at Netherfield, designed and erected by a surviving member of the crew, immediately next to the crash site. The second incident involved American flyers. The date of the crash – D-Day 6th June 1944 – is significant because there was a greater than usual air traffic on that day and therefore collisions were more likely. At about 6.00 am, two Marauder bombers collided near Battle at the cost of eleven lives: one crashed near Whatlington, the other at Ashburnham, badly damaging the great house there [it would have been much worse if both crews had not jettisoned their bombs before impact – one theory has it that one of the planes would have crashed directly on Battle if they had still been carrying their load].

There was also not inconsiderable danger from strafing by German planes. Several residents report incidents. Rosemary Bishop remembered being 'machine-gunned by a mad German pilot' on the way home from Battle and Langton School one day, and was pulled to safety into a deep ditch by her young uncle. Keith Foord's mother was in the Auxiliary Fire Service based in Hastings and one day had to dive into a shop doorway as a Messerschmitt strafed the seafront and its gun emplacements. Gina Doherty's mother was on the top deck of a bus on her way to work in

Hastings when it was strafed with the bullets along the gangway between the seats; Mr Seymour, owner of Vicary's Garage, was on his way to Winchelsea when he was strafed; and Charlotte Moore's mother told her of being strafed while in Ashburnham. George Kiloh's researches on civilian casualties concluded that in Battle and the surrounding area, 17 civilians were killed ranging in age from 14 months to 77 years old. Sometimes Spitfires were seen crashing, a memory of Robert Emeleus who saw one come down near Loose Farm at Telham, fortunately with the pilot following, attached to his parachute.

We found in our interviews that there was a grim determination in Battle to see the war through despite the many air attacks. But there was realism too: for example, Dr Eardley Davidson, so he told his family, had put cyanide capsules in the coal cellar under Martins Oak Surgery so that the family could commit suicide if the Germans had invaded.

VIP Visits

Herbert Morrison, Minister for Home Security, visited Battle on 18th September 1944 and "he expressed the thanks of the Government and of the people of London to the residents who, he said, had taken a great deal of the load off London during the flying bomb attacks ..... Mr Morrison spoke of the fine work of the local authorities and of his enormous appreciation of the fortitude and courage which the citizens of Bomb Alley had shown".

We have encountered enough reports that Winston Churchill, General Smuts and other dignitaries were driven through Battle in an open-top car, towards the coast, to say that this definitely happened. We think this may have been on 12th May 1944 because Northiam commemorates a visit by the two men, and other dignitaries, on that day, to review troops. When going through Battle they were presumably heading to the coast to inspect defences.

Preparations for D-Day

There were small but definite signs that the invasion of Normandy was imminent. Duff Hart Davis states that "all over the south of England, on roads leading to the channel coast, it became impossible for civilian traffic to move as vast military convoys were driving for five minutes, then stopping, so that the main roads were continuously blocked." Mr Seymour noted that prior to D-Day, the woods around Battle were the hiding places for what must have been thousands of troops and vehicles. D-Day and night was very noisy – wave upon wave of planes overhead and much troop activity on the roads. Douglas Lowther, reported that "the town and countryside was full of tanks and lorries and troops and then suddenly: gone! ... The sky was filled with planes: Flying Fortresses and Mitchells. They came back shot to bits, just like the film". Robert Emeleus remembers a tank which was "labouring up Marley Lane opposite Battle and Langton School."

Propaganda

Efforts to encourage the British public met with varying success. The range of leaflets about improvising to make food go further, was well designed and received but the leaflet about what to do if the invaders arrived got short shrift from the public for its vagueness and naivety.

The Germans leafleted London and the south coast with a statement of Hitler's address to the German Reichstag, calling on England to join with Germany in a historic war against Bolshevism: we have not come across one but it seems a reasonable assumption that some were dropped on Battle.

Propaganda by the British authorities was backed up by the force of law: in 1942 a woman was jailed for five years for saying that Hitler could run the country better than Churchill. One of local farmer Gerald Gay's correspondents says he thinks that the German method of ensuring full employment was more effective than Britain's: remarks which would have been close to treason in the context of the time.

An embarrassing institution in PR terms, for both sides perhaps, was the Augusta – Victoria finishing school in Bexhill which until the outbreak of war, when it closed, included among its pupils the daughters of high ranking Nazis such as Himmler, Goering and Ribbentrop. The daughters

Issued by the Ministry of Information  *in co-operation with the War Office and the Ministry of Home Security.*

If the INVADER comes

WHAT TO DO — AND HOW TO DO IT

THE Germans threaten to invade Great Britain. If they do so they will be driven out by our Navy, our Army and our Air Force. Yet the ordinary men and women of the civilian population will also have their part to play. Hitler's invasions of Poland, Holland and Belgium were greatly helped by the fact that the civilian population was taken by surprise. They did not know what to do when the moment came. *You must not be taken by surprise.* This leaflet tells you what general line you should take. More detailed instructions will be given you when the danger comes nearer. Meanwhile, read these instructions carefully and be prepared to carry them out.

I

When Holland and Belgium were invaded, the civilian population fled from their homes. They crowded on the roads, in cars, in carts, on bicycles and on foot, and so helped the enemy by preventing their own armies from advancing against the invaders. You must not allow that to happen here. Your first rule, therefore, is :—

(1) IF THE GERMANS COME, BY PARACHUTE, AEROPLANE OR SHIP, YOU MUST REMAIN WHERE YOU ARE. THE ORDER IS "STAY PUT".

If the Commander in Chief decides that the place where you live must be evacuated, he will tell you when and how to leave. Until you receive such orders you must remain where you are. If you run away, you will be exposed to far greater danger because you will be machine-gunned from the air as were civilians in Holland and Belgium, and you will also block the roads by which our own armies will advance to turn the Germans out.

II

There is another method which the Germans adopt in their invasion. They make use of the civilian population in order to create confusion and panic. They spread false rumours and issue false instructions. In order to prevent this, you should obey the second rule, which is as follows :—

(2) DO NOT BELIEVE RUMOURS AND DO NOT SPREAD THEM. WHEN YOU RECEIVE AN ORDER, MAKE QUITE SURE THAT IT IS A TRUE ORDER AND NOT A FAKED ORDER. MOST OF YOU KNOW YOUR POLICEMEN AND YOUR A.R.P. WARDENS BY SIGHT, YOU CAN TRUST THEM. IF YOU KEEP YOUR HEADS, YOU CAN ALSO TELL WHETHER A MILITARY OFFICER IS REALLY BRITISH OR ONLY PRETENDING TO BE SO. IF IN DOUBT ASK THE POLICEMAN OR THE A.R.P. WARDEN. USE YOUR COMMON SENSE.

'If the Invader Comes' leaflet

learned deportment, fitness, and how to be a member of Hitler's League of German Girls. A film *Six Minutes to Midnight*, has been made about it, starring Eddie Izzard and Judi Dench.

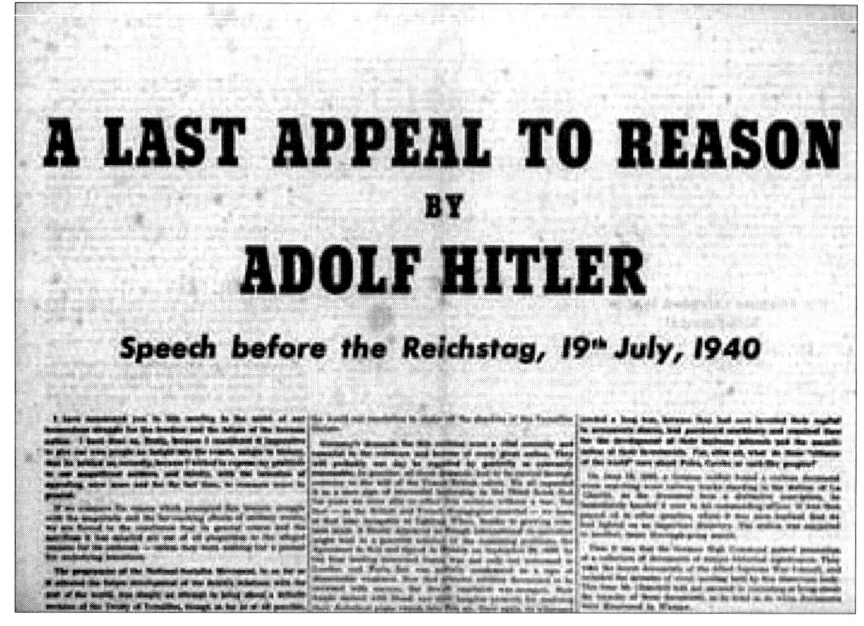

A LAST APPEAL TO REASON

BY

ADOLF HITLER

Speech before the Reichstag, 19th July, 1940

Nazi propaganda leaflet

Social Life

Dances continued in the Drill Hall throughout the war, despite the air raids and blackouts. A popular local band in the 1930s at Battle comprised Bill Nash (drums), Frank Glazier (guitar/banjo), Harry Stiles/later Les Engelfield (saxophone) and Frank Chacksfield (piano). We are indebted to Gina Doherty, a relative of Bill's, for this account. Bill had been recruited in his teens by Frank Chacksfield on Battle recreation ground around 1933/34: at that time they both lived in Wellington Gardens. He then went professional. Originally called the Rhythm Aces, the four men changed their name to the Hastorians and quickly established themselves on the circuit.

Left to right: Frank Chacksfield, Frank Glazier, Les Engelfield, Bill Nash

Our photo shows the four musicians, probably 1947. As war came, Bill joined the RAF and played in one of their Squadronnaire bands, while Frank Chacksfield's career took off as he worked with Charlie Chester and joined the 'Stars in Battledress' line-up. After the war, Frank Chacksfield specialised in broadcast work and recorded a gold disc with his big band, which he occasionally brought to Battle; his parties at Wellington Gardens are still remembered today. Bill pursued a different career but did occasional band work, sometimes helping Frank Chacksfield, scoring his musical arrangements for the *Charlie Chester Show*.

Victory in Europe

Courtesy of Lucy and Ralfe Whistler, the book cover shows the ceremony which took place on 13th May 1945, one week after VE Day, to honour the volunteers who had done so much to support Battle and the district during the course of the war. A later chapter describes the detail of that occasion.

MIKE GLAZIER: A BOYHOOD IN BATTLE 1939-45

Mike Glazier was a Battle boy in the period 1939-45. He was inspired by the RAF's Battle of Britain heroics, and by Squadron Leader John Shore MC AFC, who tells his story elsewhere in this book. So Mike joined the RAF in 1948 and specialised in the then new technologies of radar and radio communication, and software programming. He retired from the RAF in 1983 with the rank of Squadron Leader and after a period in industry, came back to Battle in 1995.

Mike Glazier

Declaration of war

Mike was in the back row of the congregation with his grandmother when, on 3rd September 1939, Dean Youard announced in St Mary's Church that war had been declared between England and Germany. The Dean was late for the start of the service – due at 11 am – having first listened to the news broadcast by Neville Chamberlain. He came in, went to the pulpit, and announced that Britain was at war with Germany. There was a short prayer and then a blast sounded on the town siren. A little later the 'all clear' sounded to show that there was no sign of enemy activity in the skies. Because ringing of church bells was to be the signal for a German invasion, this was the last day on which St Mary's bells sounded until VE Day five and a half years later. The next six months were the 'phoney war' when nothing much happened in England, apart from evacuation. Nevertheless, the sirens became a part of Battle life for the rest of the war.

Evacuation

A day or two later in September, came the mass evacuation of children from London to Battle and many other rural destinations considered safer. Mike recalls that the Battle contingent seemed mainly to come from Deptford – two girls stayed with his grandparents, one of them called Ruby.

Mike recalls that when, many years later, he was in the RAF, the wife of one of his fellow officers turned out to be one of the Battle evacuees and had fond memories of her time in the town. They were billeted to stay with local families indefinitely, but a reassessment by the Government of how safe or otherwise Sussex was, and the lack of enemy activity, caused the evacuees to be moved back to London after only a couple of months, and at any rate by December 1939. While the evacuated children were in Battle, the school day was split into two, with local children in school one half of the day and the evacuated children being taught in the other half of the day. As far as Mike remembers, there was no second wave of evacuees, as there was in some areas. On the whole the evacuees and their hosts got on well, despite the differences in background. For the London children it was a learning experience: many children, for example, had no idea what a cow was or where the food came from.

Battle on the defence: wartime precautions

Mike recalls sandbags being placed around strategic buildings in Battle as a form of defence, for example at the police station and the Watch Oak, where the Civil Defence HQ was. There was a permanent road block/ chicane in Upper Lake with concrete tubes from Rye 'Spancrete' works and barbed wire; pillboxes including one at Wellington Gardens; barricades; and anti-tank 'dragon's teeth' – these latter were around the Abbey and Deanery, by the Church hut (below) and across the field to the left, Lake Field, the Watch Oak and other places.

Tank traps by St Mary's Church

Mike recalls the Home Guard testing out the road block in a simulated exercise. Gas masks were issued. Air raid shelters were built, of brick and concrete, with a capacity of 25-30. One such shelter was at the corner of Station Road, in Mrs Bodle's garden. Such shelters were not designed to withstand a direct hit. Others were at the Abbey and Watch Oak. Anderson shelters with a concrete base, a corrugated iron top and set deep in earth, were built in private gardens where practical; where not, people were provided, for DIY assembly – with 'Morrison' table shelters (4 feet by 6 feet) from the old Gas Works yard distribution centre opposite the cinema in Lower Lake. At the Battle and Langton School, then in Marley Lane, where Mike was a pupil, the only shelter available, he says, "was a trench in the adjoining field. This trench, constructed mainly by our male parents, had its sides supported by rough timber, no overhead protection and a clay floor; it was very slippery in wet weather. I have no recollection of ever using the trench for real. There was double British Summer Time ie GMT + 2 i.e. an extra hour of daylight in the evening compared with modern summertime. This helped with harvesting and also gave people an extra hour to get home in daylight before the blackout. Windows had to be criss-crossed with sticky paper to limit shards of glass if the window shattered and at night blackouts had to be fitted to the window frames, usually made of tarred reinforced paper. This applied to schools as well as private properties. Cars had their headlights hooded at night. The blackout - enforced sometimes by a fine following inspections by the ARP Wardens - lasted until the closing months of the war." When the war was over, Mike remembered with appreciation the beautiful night skies visible during the blackout. All the signposts were removed from the roads, in case they were of use to the enemy in the event of an invasion. To some extent this was only a morale raising gesture as the Germans had been accumulating road maps of the UK for several years before the war started. The Watch Oak seems to have been the HQ of the civil defence teams but the Towers Hotel, Mike recalls, may have been the base for military defence of the area.

Rationing and salvage

Introduced in early 1940, some foods were scarce. Food and its manufacture were tightly regulated, for example the composition of the 'national loaf' – a kind of wholemeal – was determined by government. Cod liver oil and malt were given to the children of needy families and all children received a third of a pint of milk. "The only oranges we had came from a box which fell off the back of a lorry taking them into Newberys jam factory. They were Seville oranges for the making of marmalade and far too bitter to eat. They were better left where they fell."

Non-essential iron railings, including ones around graves, were removed to be melted down for the war effort. This happened to the Wesleyan chapel at the top of Station Road and to St Mary's churchyard. Later in the war, aluminium pots and pans were collected for the aircraft industry, used in construction of the new all-metal planes.

Petrol was rationed to begin with and then from 1942 was not available for private use at all. So apart from military traffic, and those like doctors and air raid services, who needed their own transport, Battle's roads were more or less empty in the second half of the war. Mike says "occasionally, when major movements of troops occurred, we had long convoys of vehicles passing through the area, usually under the control of military police on motor cycles. I particularly remember, at the start of the V1 flying bomb offensive, there was a mass movement of 3.7 inch 'ack ack' anti-aircraft guns from the London area down to the coast."

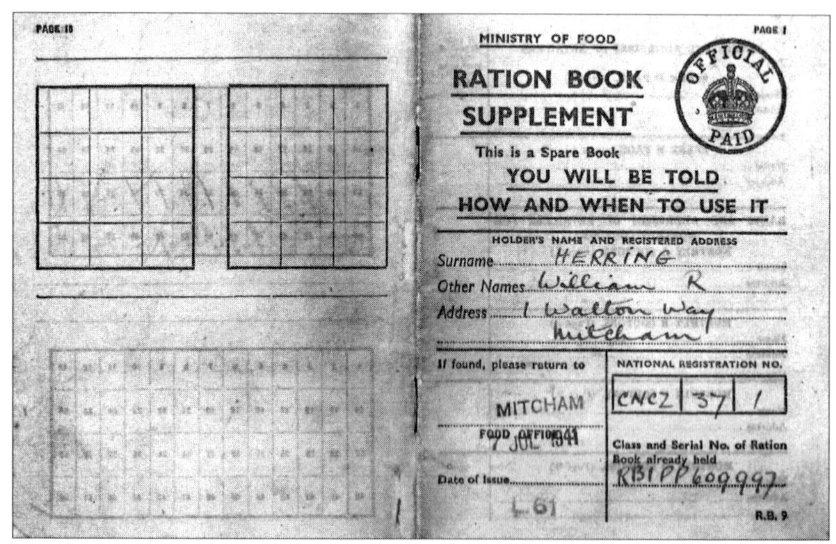
PAGE 1

MINISTRY OF FOOD

RATION BOOK SUPPLEMENT

OFFICIAL PAID

This is a Spare Book

YOU WILL BE TOLD HOW AND WHEN TO USE IT

HOLDER'S NAME AND REGISTERED ADDRESS

Surname HERRING

Other Names William R

Address 1 Walton Way Mitcham

If found, please return to MITCHAM FOOD OFFICE

7 JUL 1941

Date of Issue

L 61

NATIONAL REGISTRATION NO. CNCZ 37 1

Class and Serial No. of Ration Book already held RB1 PP 609997

R.B. 9

Ration book cover

Mike plays down the impact of the food rationing: "I don't remember ever being hungry during the war – food was of necessity rather plain but still nutritious. Practically everyone fully embraced the slogan of 'Dig for Victory'. That said, you were lucky to get a rasher of bacon a week. So Battle people, who had been used to growing their own food, grew more. Allotments which had been neglected and overgrown were soon cleared and in full cultivation. We had two 10 rod[1] patches plus our cottage garden and so were reasonably self-sufficient for vegetables and fruits. We also kept chicken and pet rabbits to eke out our meat ration. The butcher would come round to dispose of them. We learned to eat what was put in front of us and not to waste any food."

"Children helped the war effort in various ways. We collected hips for rose hip syrup and sheep wool from brambles and barbed wire. The wool was processed for use in factories to mop up oil. We also collected blackberries to sell to the jam factory. Another source of income was returning jam jars for reuse. Another source of income for my brother and me, although not really in direct support of the war effort, was the collection of chestnuts and mushrooms. Lorry drivers who had cause to visit London, would sell them for us in pubs down the Old Kent Road. I suppose we could claim to be helping in food production!"

Mike recalls that workers in certain occupations, for example the rescue services and the gypsum mines, got enhanced food rations.

Schools and education

Following the German blitzkrieg through Holland, Belgium and France in May 1940, leading to the Dunkirk evacuation of the British Expeditionary Force, the invasion of Britain seemed a real threat. Children from the coastal towns were evacuated, for example pupils from Hastings Grammar went to St Albans, but this was not done in Battle.. In Battle, only the pupils from the Abbey School and those attending Bexhill Grammar School, left the area – the rest of the town's schoolchildren stayed put.

1 A rod is just over 5 metres

For schoolchildren who remained in Battle, there were changes: the male teachers left for the armed services; the senior boys aged 12-13 cultivated the caretaker's garden under the slogan 'Dig for Victory'; and lessons were often disrupted by enemy activity.

With the advent of the flying bomb offensive in June 1944, and the tactic of preventing them from reaching London, there was a greater chance that our area would be more affected than before. (This proved correct with 374 flying bombs downed in the Battle Rural District.) In view of the perceived threat, at Battle and Langton School watchers were placed in the front playground at the two entrances. These roles were performed on a rota basis from boys in the senior class. At the first sign of danger they had to respond by running the length of the corridors blowing a whistle, whereupon pupils and teachers were to take cover under their desks. One afternoon, such an alert occurred. Mike says "Ernie Hussey, a fairly hefty lad, was warden on the senior school corridor. After the necessary blasts of the whistle, he ran into our classroom and dived under the teacher's desk, rather than take time to reach his own desk. There wasn't room for Ernie and Mrs Clarke, the Headmaster's wife who was unceremoniously propelled from her position of relative safety. Ernie's panic was due to a flying bomb heading towards the school. Fortunately a pilot in a pursuing fighter managed to tip the bomb's wing, so deflecting it eventually to fall alongside the sewage plant, only a few hundred yards as the crow flies, from the school."

"Unexploded ordnance", Mike continues, "posed a very real threat. At school we were lectured on the hazard and warned never to touch. The threat came not only from the bombing with incendiary and high explosive devices. They also dropped anti-personnel bombs, for example butterfly bombs. Crashed aircraft quite often resulted in unexploded bullets and shells being scattered around. Also it was inevitable that military exercises would lead to the loss of all sorts of explosive devices for example 2 inch mortar rounds. Even with all the warnings, 'lads will be lads'. The charge from five 303 rifle bullets provided the fillings for home made fireworks. Unfortunately one of our number had a damaged hand after his body heat caused a mercury fuse to detonate. Another hazard was created by the cables dangling from barrage balloons (pictured). We were told that somewhere in the area someone had been killed when a cable he was hanging on to came into contact with the overhead high voltage feeder."

Barrage balloon

The military

Shortly after the declaration of war, a Territorial Army unit arrived in the area with searchlights, one of which was deployed at the lower end of Marley Lane. This unit was mainly comprised of workers from the Greenwich Gas Works. Shortly after a large contingent of the Devonshire Regiment arrived in Battle. Mike continues: "I remember that during a Parade outside St Mary's Church, a little lad was marooned on the high pavement and the RSM, without breaking step, scooped him up and deposited him on the other side of the road with his mother. His action drew a round of applause for the RSM from the watching crowd." Early in 1940 the Devonshires were replaced by Canadians who took over the Abbey as their local HQ and were billeted in Battle Abbey School with a large encampment to the rear. "They spoilt us kids with sweets and oranges" recalls Mike, "we like many families had them home for meals." The local bus garage opposite to what was then the Senlac cinema, was used to service their vehicles. The boys would hang around seeing what was going on and were given rides through the woods on test drives in bren carriers. But many of the Canadians at Battle were never seen again after the disastrous raid on German-occupied Dieppe in August 1942: over 80% of the 6000 Allied troops in the operation were Canadian; 60% of that Allied force were killed, wounded or captured. "The loss of many good Canadian friends, particularly one called Con, on the Dieppe Raid really brought home to me for the first time the horror of war."

It was in 1942 when the Americans made their first appearance in the Battle area, when they set up a huge radio station at Home Corner, Catsfield.

Mike remembers the Towers Hotel being commandeered as an HQ for some form of war use.[2]

Home Guard and other voluntary services

Mike recalls the Home Guard working closely with the military once they had their weapons. They were on duty every night. The Battle Home Guard was quite diverse in its membership, with, for example, the manager of a furniture business, a postman, a miner and a firework maker, being among the members. The Captain of the Battle Home Guard, was Percy Woodhams, who was the person who ran Battle cattle market and then lived in what is now the Bull pub.

Towards the end of the war, the Home Guard held an open day in the Abbey where they displayed their weapons: besides pistols, rifles and sten guns, they also had anti- tank guns and mortars.

The person in charge of the local army cadet unit was Jock Purvis, the hairdresser in Mount Street, who would never charge young cadets for their haircut. A 'character and a half', he had been a PoW in the First World War, put to work in salt mines.

2 Canadian Royal Engineers

Battle Home Guard in Market area of the town
Top row left to right: Norman Oliver, "Farmer"Taylor, Adams? "Dusty" Pocock, Barnes, unknown, Freer, unknown, Alan Ballard, John Humphreys, Basil "Tubby" Martin, Joe Patterson
Bottom row left to right: Lt/Cpl Cliff Pocock, Cpl Eldridge, Sgt Arthur Day, Sgt George Reid, Lt Rex Hubbard, Sgt Len Larby, Sgt George Barrett, Cpl Wibley, Cpl Brooks, Cpl Goodsell

Mike's father served in the local rescue service (led by George Bramley), whose activities are described in 'Tin Hat', a contemporary Battle based informal magazine for voluntary services, discovered in the BDHS archives. "This often harrowing job involved not only dealing with the results of bombing but also with crashed aircraft and removal of bodies from them. Because of his small stature and practical knowledge of building construction and plumbing, my father's speciality was in tunnelling to reach trapped casualties."

Women's Land Army: 'Lumber Jills'

'Sometime in 1943/44 a team of Lumber Jills[3] descended on the wood to the left hand side of Powdermill Lane from its start down to the first field. They commenced felling all the Scots pines. Led by a male, the team had

3 Forestry Division of the Women's Land Army

half a dozen girls in it. They had no mechanical aids apart from a tractor and swung huge axes to prime the cut then trim the felled timber. Large two-handed saws were used to make the final cut, with the girls working on their knees. Once felled and trimmed of all branches, the trees were cut to the required length to be used as pit props. We benefitted from their efforts in collecting the branches, to be used on our home fires, and thus supplement our coal supplies."

Squadron Leader John Shore MC AFC

Mike remembers him (when a Wing Commander) as the local hero, taking the salute at a military parade outside St Mary's Church. Mike described the location of Mr Shore Senior's bungalow Two Oaks off North Trade Road where he would sit outside – he was wheelchair-bound. He had a miner's lamp which Mike had polished for him. Mr Shore Senior had been some kind of explosives expert in the First World War and then ran a garage off the Canadia Road. John Shore had joined the RAF on a short service commission in 1936, having spent a couple of years working in Peter Seymour's garage. His account of his "home run" is elsewhere in this book.

'Lumber Jills'

Returning British POWs

Mike recalls the decorations in Wellington Gardens - and particularly on his parents' house at No 24 – to welcome home Rex Pearson from his four years in German captivity. In less than a year Mike's family moved into No 25 Wellington Gardens and they got to know Rex and family more intimately. Another returning POW was Stanley Apps, whose family lived in Senlac Gardens.

Battle of Britain

Mike recalls that the Battle of Britain was an exciting time for children, watching the dogfights and collecting souvenirs from crashed aircraft. In particular he recalls an incident when a "crashed Heinkel HE 111 (shown below) had been recovered on a 'queen mary' long loader which had got stuck in the narrow bends and high banking at the bottom of Powdermill Lane. Sufficient of the main wing had not been removed and thus protruded from the sides of the vehicle. Whilst collecting our trophies – coloured wiring and Perspex glass with which to make bracelets and rings- and ably assisted by the RAF lads, we heard the whistle of descending bombs. Everyone took shelter under the 'queen mary' – the bombs dropped about a quarter of a mile away by the iron bridge over the railway on the Crowhurst Road."

Heinkel 111 Bundesarchiv Bild 1011-401-0244-27 (Goricke)

"The majority of Allied pilots who crashed during the Battle of Britain were British, supported by pilots from all countries of the Empire. There were also a few from countries in Europe, who had escaped the German invasion of their homelands. There were French, Poles and Czechs, some of them having their own squadrons. German aircrews were of course detained sometimes by members of the public. In fact one of our teachers and her mother made such an arrest in Hastings."

Bombing

"One night early in 1940, four bombs exploded in the Pound Field and Blackmans Field, very adjacent to the railway line and less than half a mile from Battle Hill Bridge. It was even closer to our house in Chapel Cottages but didn't cause us any damage. I think that event was the first time that bombs had dropped on Battle. I vividly remember the massed squadrons of German bombers, passing overhead towards London and others of our cities, with their con-trails lit by the setting sun. Whilst this was all very exciting for us youngsters I know that it was far from that for our parents. I remember my mother spending many a night watching and listening for the raiders on their return journey. She wouldn't get into bed until the all-clear sounded. During this period my father was seldom at home at night. He was a member of the ARP rescue team and spent most nights on duty at the Watch Oak."

The wide distribution of bombs across East Sussex arose from them being jettisoned after failure to release them in that day's mission.

The community spirit of Battle remained- for example if children were stranded when the air raid sirens began, they would be taken in by the nearest householder. So it was that on one occasion Mike was sheltered in the headmaster's house in Marley Lane, pushed under his stairs, the safest part of the house.

Throughout 1942 air activity continued. Anti-personnel butterfly bombs were used, says Mike. "I only heard of one casualty: a road worker killed in one of the outlying villages."

1943 was the year when the Allies began to assert some superiority over the Germans, who Mike says, "switched tactics, replacing massive raids with hit and run raids along the Channel coast. Groups of fighter bombers would approach, flying just above the waves to defeat the radar cover and achieve surprise. Each carried one bomb and caused more mayhem by machine-gunning any target they could find. Most raids were on the coastal towns but Battle did receive a visit in February 1943, the results of which are well documented." Mike does not know whether this raid had a specific target in mind, possibly the Senlac Works which was making some kind of military hardware; or perhaps the concentration of Canadian troops at the Abbey."

One of the largest bombs dropped, Mike recalls, landed by the lane to Little Hemingfold Farm at Telham. It made the biggest crater that Mike and his friends had ever seen.

"A week after D-Day the Germans launched the V1 flying bomb offensive. There were corridors over and adjacent to Battle so we saw plenty of them', says Mike. 'Almost as soon as this offensive started, a large number of 3.7 in 'ack ack' guns which had surrounded London were moved to the coast, many of them passing through Battle. The tactic to defeat these "buzz bombs" as we called them, was for the fighters to attack them over the sea, the guns to take over at the coast, then the fighters to take over again, with barrage balloons as the final defensive ring.V1s came down in Battle parish, one in Tumble Down near the railway line, one adjacent to the sewage farm off Marley Lane, and one behind the Watch Oak. There were no serious casualties."

Mike remembers the following consequence of the bombing for the housing stock: "In 1944, because of the large number of damaged residential properties in and around London, some local building tradesmen were drafted in to help with the repair task. I remember my uncle worked in Croydon for several months."

Operation Market Garden

"Earlier in the war, we had marvelled at the masses of German aircraft passing overhead for the huge raids on our cities and we never expected to see so many aircraft at one and the same time again. That was until Operation Market Garden, the Allied airborne landing at Arnhem[4]. The skies above Battle were filled by a constant stream of Dakotas towing gliders, which seemed to go on for ever. I think that there were two waves of aircraft on successive days. Unfortunately Market Garden was not the success we had hoped for and the Dutch had to suffer another winter of occupation and a terrible shortage of food. The situation for them was so dire that in the closing days of the war, the Swedish Red Cross delivered some barges of food without the agreement of the Germans. In addition our government told the Germans that Bomber Command and the American 6th Air Force would be flying special missions to drop hampers of food, on defined routes and heights. There was no attempt to interfere with the missions. Years later I was serving in a NATO post and shared an office with a Dutch Major who as a 14 year-old had benefitted from our bombing them with food."

German PoWs

The Italian prisoners were based at Robertsbridge and were allowed out after Italy made peace in 1944. The German PoWs at Normanhurst however remained confined until after the war ended. The German PoWs put on musical concerts in aid of rebuilding the then Hastings Hospital which they has bombed. Mike remembers vividly their unaccompanied rendition of *Silent Night* at St Mary's, Battle at Christmas; "and many years later in 1970, when on a business trip to Germany, meeting up with a former member of that PoW choir. He spoke fondly of his time at the Normanhurst camp and enquired if Mr Lee was still the butcher and Mr Hickmot still a policeman. A charge could not be levied for attendance at the PoW concerts but a silver collection was made. It was listening to their rendition of parts from the William Tell and Poet and Peasant overtures that ignited my love of classical music. Many of the younger children had toys carved by the German prisoners. One was a bat like that used for table tennis but with a hole in the middle. Around the outside were mounted

4 September 1944

four chickens with lines attached which passed through the centre hole and were tied to a weight which when swung caused the chickens in turn to peck for food. Another toy was a clown on a trapeze which, when the side poles were squeezed, caused the clown to perform somersaults."

D Day preparations

Mike recalls that the Dieppe raid indicated to allies and Germany alike that the invasion of Europe was on the cards – it was just a matter of when and where; the Germans believed the target would be the Pas de Calais. The ill-fated allied landing exercise off the Devon coast, sabotaged by German E boats with the loss of 1,000 lives, also added to the expectation that something would be attempted. All through early 1944 there was a build-up of supplies to support the impending invasion of Europe. Mike and his young friends spotted that to this end a large petrol storage facility was created at Powdermill Lane towards the Abbey pond under cover of some oaks. Concrete bases were put down with tin sides onto which were stacked 4 gallon drums of American design. For several weeks a fleet of dumper trucks transferred the full cans from the railway sidings- living at the top of Station Road Mike and his family had a grandstand view of this activity. At the end of May 1944 the majority of the Canadians moved out to their assembly points for D-Day – Operation Overlord.

Rumours of Death Rays

"In times of war, with the need to maintain secrecy on everyone's mind, it was inevitable that rumours are started and further enhanced in their retelling. Thus it was that early in the war there was all sorts of speculation as to what the installation on Pevensey Marsh was for, with three 330 foot masts on one side of the road and four 240 foot masts on the other. One tale going the rounds was that its rays could stop all motor traffic, but the one most favoured by us lads was that it was capable of emitting a death ray. In truth it was one in a chain of radar stations: without their early warnings of impending air attacks the Battle of Britain may well have been lost. It is rather ironic that some ten years later, in 1952, I had the opportunity to climb those towers. I was a young corporal in charge of the team installing the VHF communication transmitter and receiver buildings in Hooe village for the new underground control facility at Wartling."

Wartime radar station

VIP visits

Mike is sure that, perched as he was on a pillar outside the old gasworks yard and opposite the Senlac cinema, now Burstow and Hewett, that he saw an open-top car with Churchill and General Smuts in it, pass through Lower Lake in the weeks before D-Day, during a fine afternoon . This might be a continuation of the recorded visit made to Northiam on 12th May 1944, to review troops.

VE Day Tuesday 8 May 1945

Mike, then 14, heard the news of Victory in Europe when taking a French lesson on a sunny day in Bexhill Grammar School. Directly outside our classroom, the Head was telling the Deputy that the surrender was to take place the following day. Hearing such momentous news Mike shouted out to inform the whole class, only to have a board rubber thrown at him by Mr Ruffhead (a character who had fought for the International Brigade in the Spanish Civil War) for indiscipline. At home, Mike's father and he were invited by Mr Cradock (owner of Pepering Eye Farm) – for whom Mike's father was building a brick fireplace- to go to the Railway Inn at Senlac. Once there, Mike had a pint of beer, which made him very ill. He has avoided beer ever since! The celebrations, though, were tempered a little because there were still some local men who were prisoners in Japan.

Adapting to peace

Generally returning servicemen adjusted back into civilian life as well as could be expected, but Mike recalls that there were some difficulties, particularly where a wife had been unfaithful or a girlfriend had married another. Several of the troops billeted in Battle married local girls and settled down to family life in the local area. They could usually be identified by their conspicuous accents. Some local girls who had married visiting troops, moved to their husband's home overseas. This included those who married Canadians. Joyce Adams (now Gaudreau) who lived alongside Mike and his family in Chapel Cottages, was one of the latter.

RICHARD MOORE - THE VIEW FROM HANCOX

"I was 8 when the war began, living at Hancox, Whatlington (East Sussex) but during term time my elder sister Hilary and I went to Caldbec House each weekday where we were taught by a governess, Miss Maurice (succeeded by Miss Pembroke in 1940, both very good teachers and good people) together with Benedicta Whistler, her brother Ralfe (who now lives at The Dodo House), Ian Fraser (whose home was Campfield House near Powdermills) and Audrey Markby who lived at West Court, Caldbec Hill.

The Outbreak of War

In my family there was a difference of opinion between the generations about how they regarded the prospect of war. At lunch on 1st September 1939, when Germany invaded Poland and two days before Great Britain declared war, I, like many small boys, imagined war to be exciting and secretly looked forward to it, said "I'm glad it's happened. We know where we are now." My father, who was carving mutton and who served as a surgeon in the Royal Navy from 1914-19 and whose brother Gillachrist, a Second Lieutenant in the Royal Sussex Regiment, was killed at the First Battle of Ypres on 7th November 1914, was annoyed. He said something like "That's wrong; war is dreadful." My brother, who was in the Officer's Training Corps at Eton and who, at 16, was near to calling-up age and had realised that we had to stop Hitler, said he agreed with me.

For the Moores the day war was declared had an element of farce. At Hancox five girl evacuees and their teacher from Greenwich High School, Miss Parry, had arrived a few days before. On Sunday morning they all went with my elder sister to a children's service at Whatlington Church. I had a stomach upset and stayed at home. Hilary told me that, in the middle of the service, just after 11.00 am., Kitty Muggeridge (the wife of Malcolm Muggeridge – both then keen atheists) rushed into the church and spoke to Mr Browell, a retired clergyman who lived in Whatlington and was taking the service. He told the children to return home or, in the case of the evacuees, to the houses where they had been billeted. When Hilary asked a grown up why they had to go back to Hancox she was told it was because: "the cows had got out". Really it was because of the declaration of war. The cows would not have frightened the country children nor the evacuees at Hancox, who were a sturdy lot, so it was a silly reason to give. In fact the children need not have been disturbed but many people expected to be bombed immediately the war began. Sure enough the air raid siren went off within minutes. But this alarm was a nation-wide occurrence, caused, it turned out, by a mistaken identification of a British plane flying (we heard later) over the Firth of Forth.

Preparations for Air Raids

Alarm about air raids began years before the war. It was thought that "the bomber will always get through" and the destruction of Guernica in the Spanish Civil War by the German air force shocked the democratic world. From the Munich Crisis of September 1938 Air Raid Precautions began to be taken. Gas masks were issued to all civilians and carried in cardboard boxes. For small children gas masks designed to look like Mickey Mouse were issued. My younger sister, Meriel, who was 2¾ when war began, had one. Babies had masks which enclosed them.

Gas had been used from the Second Battle of Ypres in April 1915 with horrific effects which made people dread its use on civilians. In fact it was never used militarily in the Second World War. It was used by the Nazis to murder Jews, gypsies and other prisoners in concentration camps, and in Nazi sealed lorries in the Soviet Union from 1941. But these horrors were known by few British 'till 1945, although we knew Jews were being murdered in huge numbers. At the beginning of the War the British and French promised not to use gas unless the Germans did first. Since the prevailing winds were more West to East than vice versa this deterrent worked. I remember hearing it repeated on the BBC by the British and American governments in 1943 I think.

Gas mask practice at Caldbec House

In the first few weeks of the War we had to carry our gas masks whenever we left our homes. This was given up quite quickly and we kept our gas masks at home. Another precaution soon not taken in the Battle area and I think in most rural districts, was to go into air raid shelters when the air raid warning wailed. Many people had air raid shelters dug in their gardens. At Hancox extra wooden pillars to support the ceiling were put into the wine cellar. We kept some food in the cellar in case the house collapsed and we were trapped. The shelters were not much used because Battle was never bombed intensively and during the Battle of Britain most people preferred to watch the 'dog fights' as fights between airplanes were called.

One Air Raid Precaution that was strictly enforced from 3rd September 1939 until about 24th April 1945 (a few days before the War in Europe ended) was the black-out. Every window had to be covered so that no light leaked out which would show the enemy where there were targets. Enforcing this was one of the main duties of the Air Raid Wardens who patrolled at night wearing white tin hats with ARP painted on them. I remember quite late in the War somebody left the light on in an upstairs room in Hancox and my father was fined £1 (about £50 now). At the beginning of the War even vehicles at night could show no lights but this caused so many deaths and injuries in road accidents that, after a few weeks, cars, motor bikes and other vehicles carried subdued lights. Curiously I don't remember whether this applied to bicycles.

Evacuees & Refugees

After about two months when no air raids occurred, the evacuees mostly returned to London and other cities. In 1940 when the Blitz made living in London and big provincial towns really dangerous, evacuation began again but not to Sussex and Kent which were then in the front line. We were sorry when the 5 evacuees and their teacher left. They were all nice girls and so was Miss Parry. I think they enjoyed a taste of rural life: the hop picking which began a few days after the outbreak of war (the wonderful smell of the hops being roasted in the oast houses is something I miss to this day) and the farm animals. My sister taught one of the girls to ride on Hilary's Welsh pony. The girls must have been homesick sometimes but I remember them as cheerful. They were generous in playing with me who was at least four years younger. I remember they put on a gymnastic display on the front lawn. Just before the War there had been much excitement about the first successful birth of quintuplets which took place in Canada. This I think was one of the reasons why we called the evacuees 'the quins', although of course we used their Christian names when speaking to them individually.

In the years before 1939 and especially after the state-sponsored '*Kristallnacht*' persecution of 9th-10th November 1938, the awful position of Jews in Germany became increasingly clear for them.

Not that British opinion was welcoming to Jewish refugees in all quarters, as I recall my mother telling me. This was partly due to some anti-Semitism, partly because unemployment was high, and there was also a fear of enemy aliens. When the first '*Kindertransport*' child refugees arrived from Austria and from neighbouring Czechoslovakia (organised on his own initiative by the British Consul in Prague), the *Daily Mail* went as far as to headline their arrival as a 'Disgrace to England' and an 'outrage'.

Aftermath of Kristallnacht, Germany 1938

But my mother, Mary Moore, was a serious but broad-minded Anglican (she had a *prie-dieu* prayer desk in her room) and was a friend of Bishop Bell of Chichester. His predecessor as Bishop of Chichester, Winfred Burrows, was my maternal grandfather. Bishop Bell, who from the outset worked with German anti-Nazi resistance, was a great friend of its leading light, Dietrich Bonnhoefer. Bell was particularly concerned with the difficulties of German Jews who had married gentiles. The gentiles were helped by the Red Cross but to come to Britain the Jews had to have a close family relation already resident or have a pre-existing job offer.

Mary Moore took a strong line on helping the Jewish refugees: she respected Jewish learning especially in the sciences and philosophy; remembered that Jesus and the apostles were Jews, and believed that the horrible persecution of minorities should always be opposed. So my parents decided to do something about it. They began by taking in a charming Kindertransport girl of 15 from Hamburg who stayed a fortnight in the Spring before being sent to a Jewish family. Next, on a longer term basis from August 1939, they took into Hancox Gerhard and Helene Israel and their two children, Hildegard and Margot. They were among the last to get out of Germany. The Nazis had tried to force Helene, a gentile, to divorce Gerhard on the grounds of racial purity. She had refused so the family was persecuted and in great danger. Their daughters, Hildegard aged 7 and Margot 4, probably had to endure the horrible practice in state schools of having to line up with the gentile children for school milk. When they reached the head of the queue, they were told 'No milk for Jewish pigs'.

"GERMAN JEWS POURING INTO THIS COUNTRY"

By Daily Mail Reporter

"The way stateless Jews from Germany are pouring in from every port of this country is becoming an outrage. I intend to enforce the law to the fullest."

In these words, Mr. Herbert Metcalfe, the Old-street magistrate yesterday referred to the number of aliens entering this country through the "back door"—a problem to which *The Daily Mail* has repeatedly pointed.

Soon Caught

The number of aliens entering this country can be seen by the number of prosecutions in recent months. It is very difficult for the alien to escape the increasing vigilance of the police and port authorities.

Even if aliens manage to break through the defences it is not long before they are caught and deported.

The greatest of their difficulties is employment. Every employer must

address as the other three, was discharged under the Summary Jurisdiction Act. She had been charged with knowingly harbouring Bockner.

Mr. Metcalfe said it was clear that she relied on Bockner, for she had consented to marry him. He had no reason to doubt her story.

It was stated that Bockner was born at Minsk, Russia. Flerman was born in Warsaw, and had stated that he had been married to Weiss according to Jewish rites.

Mr. Clifford Watts, who appeared for all three, said he was instructed that they were making their way to friends in Africa when arrested.

Flerman and Weiss, who was expecting to become a mother in some months, could leave this country if the magistrate would give them an opportunity.

Flerman, he added, had had to run away from Berlin. He was a Jew, and he met Weiss, who was born there. Her brother was arrested and shot.

Example of adverse media coverage of German Jews entering UK 1938

The Israel family arrived at Hancox on 9th August 1939. Hildegard was like Gretel in the fairy story, sturdy with long blonde plaits. Margot was of conventionally Jewish appearance, dark with no plaits. The Israels stayed with us until February 1940 and eventually started a new life in Canada. So that the Israels could be admitted to this country, my parents had to give them jobs. Mrs. Israel was employed as a cook and Mr Israel as a handyman (he was described officially as a butler). In fact we already had a cook, May Buckwell, and her husband Jesse Buckwell was the gardener who could turn his hand to many things. They started at Hancox in the early 1930s or perhaps earlier and stayed until the end of the War. Mr Israel made a sledge with a seat so that my sister and I could be towed through snow.

My father, Sir Alan Moore, was Medical Officer of Health (MOH) for the area and was on the Emergency Committee (of Battle Rural District Council) which basically ran Battle in the Second World War. The Committee met at the Watch Oak, then the civil defence HQ for Battle. They met every night by rota but were permanently on call in the event of invasion, mass casualties or other disasters. As MOH, my father was responsible in Battle for: public health, school inspections, medical supplies, the effectiveness of the nursing service, and medical inspections. He had to interview any overseas refugees arriving at Rye and other nearby ports, and, working with the Women's Voluntary Service (WVS), deal with health issues e.g. scabies and lack of house training among a significant minority of the thousands of young evacuees in the Battle area. The WVS not only provided food for the evacuated children, they also dealt with many issues arising from the large-scale re-settlement of children into a rural area. Some of the children came from city slums where life was utterly different. Rumours of children defecating in rooms got around the country and tense situations sometimes arose when residents on whom children were billeted found them dirty or unattractive and refused to take them.

I recall a notable incident when my father had to deal with a boatload of Dutch refugees who arrived at Rye on 15th May 1940, five days after the German attack on France, the Netherlands, Belgium and Luxembourg. He took me with him and arrived at Rye Harbour to find a private yacht with the owner and his wife, two crew and a sailor they had picked up after his trawler hit a mine. The woman repeated over and over again the phrase: "Rotterdam flat, flat, flat" moving her arms horizontally, and so it was. Some 1,000 inhabitants of Rotterdam had perished in the German attack, the wooden houses having burned like tinder. Holland surrendered when the Germans threatened to do the same to Amsterdam.

At about the same time I remember hearing the story of a Dutch warship which had escaped the German attack and had made its way to Chatham, although its radio system had been knocked out. The Dutch captain disembarked and rang the Admiralty from a public callbox to explain that: "Captain Van Tromp and his Royal Netherlands warship are at Chatham." The Admiralty officer who took the call (remembering the Dutch attack up the Medway of 1667) replied: "Oh no, not again!" This delighted the Dutch.

Dunkirk and the Fall of France

After the enemy invaded France and the Benelux countries on 10th May 1940, the German army soon routed the French and British armies in spite of brave resistance, especially at Lille by the French and by the British at Calais. I remember going to a Red Cross fete at Crowham Manor in Westfield in May. I noticed how the adults lowered their voices when talking about the War situation when children were near them. At the end of May until 3rd June the Dunkirk evacuation took place. My parents, going to the wedding in London of my cousin Matthew Pryor, had to change trains at Tunbridge Wells. A long train, full of British and French soldiers from Dunkirk pulled into the station. My parents and the other civilians on the platform bought them tea. Soon after this I was in Hastings and saw on an evening newspaper placard 'Germans at the gates of Paris'. For the first time in the War I felt the chill of fear and real anxiety.

The Home Guard

At this time the Home Guard was formed. At Whatlington my father was the oldest (aged 58) and my brother, who had been in the Home Guard at Eton until the end of term, the youngest at 17. At first they only had armbands with LDV (Local Defence Volunteers) on them. The LDV was what they were called until Churchill soon changed their name to the much more inspiring Home Guard. For arms they only had any shotguns that they owned. My father also took an ancient pike [pictured below] we had at Hancox, which had been surrendered to ancestors following the suppression of the 1798 rebellion in Ireland. It originally came from one of the ships of the Spanish Armada wrecked off the Irish coast. Its staff was only about half its original length. My mother asked my father why he was taking this obsolete weapon. My father replied: "If one of these parachutists (much used in the German invasion of the Netherlands) is coming down, I can stick him up with it."

Richard Moore and the pike used by the Home Guard

The Whatlington Home Guard used to go on a hillock on the southern side of the Riccards Lane and Stream Lane cross roads every night. A single German with a sub-machine gun could easily have killed them all. Quite soon they got rifles and ill-fitting khaki uniforms and tin hats.

Once the threat of invasion was serious, metal frames were erected in flat fields to stop German gliders from landing. All signposts were removed so that invaders would not know where they were. Concrete machine gun posts were built as soon as possible (you can see one in the grounds of Bodiam Castle). Lots of big concrete blocks were put up round the edges of fields to stop or at least delay tanks. A lot of them could be seen from Swales Green until very recently.

After the threat of invasion became real in May 1940 or perhaps earlier, church bells were not allowed to be rung unless invaders arrived. One day in August or September Mr Buckwell the gardener came into the kitchen in Hancox where his wife was cooking breakfast. He said: "The bells are ringing. The Germans have landed."

"I've no breakfast for them" said Mrs Buckwell. It was of course a false alarm.

After the fall of France in June 1940 my sister and I and our nurse were evacuated to Pilton Manor where a second cousin of my mother's (Amy Bond) lived. It is near Glastonbury and was a handsome house with a big farm. The eldest son and daughter were already in the services – he in the Army, she in the Wrens, as the women in the Navy were called. I remember being impressed by the smartness of her uniform.

After six weeks we were brought back to Hancox. Although they never told me this, I think my parents found the anxiety of being separated worse than the anxiety of air attacks. The day after we got back home, Goering ordered the Luftwaffe to begin its mass attack and the main part of the Battle of Britain began.

The Battle of Britain

On 13th August, after Ralfe Whistler's birthday, I went to Caldbec House. Soon we heard a loud continuous roar so Ralfe and I went into the garden, lay under a bush and peeped out. We counted 400 German planes. They were largely Heinkel IIIs which had transparent noses in which the bomb aimer lay. We could see the men quite easily and also the pilots in other types of aircraft like the Junker 88s. I believe the Germans never flew so low again because the RAF swooped on them from above and they had too little room to take evasive action.

Until the end of October we saw 'dog fights' about every other day. When I see vapour trails in the sky of aircraft flying to Gatwick, I am always reminded of the Battle of Britain. Once I was at Caldbec House and saw, quite low down, a Junkers 88 being attacked by two British fighters. Smoke was coming out of the German plane and suddenly it crashed into the ground about three miles away and blew up. It landed near Cripps Corner. Raymond Elphick, the teenage son of the man who kept the Whatlington Garage, visited the scene and brought back the leather sleeve of one of the crew. When he looked he could not see through. Part of the German's arm was still in it. I collected some less grisly relics, bits of the plane, a few days later.

At the end of October my mother and I were out gathering nuts in a field near Hancox. A 'dog fight' involving many planes began over us and a large bit of fabric covering part of a plane floated down and landed at my feet. My brother picked up part of a German map which showed part of the Midlands with markings in red. He handed it in to the military.

He and my mother were walking in Ashburnham Park when a German plane swooped down and machine gunned them. They took shelter in a wood. Once I was out rabbiting with him in a field, the Thirteen Acre, at Hancox. He had a shot gun and I a bag to carry home any rabbits or pigeons he shot. Suddenly a German plane swooped down and flew slowly and low, apparently looking for prey. We plunged into a ditch between two fields and hid there until he flew away.

It was widely believed that German paratroops had landed in disguise especially in the Netherlands. One day my sister Hilary, in Hastings with my mother, observed some nuns sitting in chairs on the Front knitting. My sister said: "I wonder if that is really a nun. She is knitting very badly."

I remember that on September 15th, which is still celebrated as Battle of Britain Day with a service in Westminster Abbey, there was a great deal of activity in the air. The next day I went down to the drawing room at Hancox to listen to the 7.00 am. news on the wireless. The BBC announced that 175 German planes had been shot down on the 15th. I listened to the 8.00 am. bulletin: the score had gone up to 185. Though this was later found to be very inaccurate, the true figure was I think only 52, the RAF lost very few and it was a turning point. Up till then the Luftwaffe had concentrated on bombing the RAF bases in Sussex and Kent, like Tangmere near Chichester and Biggin Hill. They knew that if they could put these bases out of action, they could gain control of the air over the South East. The Hurricanes and Spitfires, though better fighter planes than anything the Germans had, had a very short range. If they had had to take off and land from East Anglia, let alone further north, they could only have been over the South East for about half an hour. The Luftwaffe flying from bases 20 to 40 miles from the English coast would have had a huge advantage. Happily their losses were so heavy compared with the RAF's that Goering, the Commander in Chief of the German air force, lost his nerve and switched to terror bombing of London and other big cities. This killed many civilians, about 25,000 in London alone, until the heavy bombing raids ended on 10th May 1941 when the Chamber of the House of Commons and much else was destroyed. Thereafter the Germans concentrated on preparing for the invasion of the Soviet Union on 22nd June 1941.

In late 1940 London was bombed for 56 consecutive nights. We could often hear the bombers flying en masse and high on the way to London. They came back much less in mass formation.

My last memory of 1940, the country's 'finest hour', was of 29th December which was savagely cold, the water sometimes froze in the London firemen's hoses. Some time before midnight our nurse came into my bedroom and told me to look out of my window. The bedroom light was turned off while I pulled back the blackout curtains. To the North the whole sky was red. It was London burning 50 miles away.

Butterfly Bombs & Doodle Bugs

Nothing in the war exceeded the excitement of having a grandstand view of the Battle of Britain, but Battle and district saw a lot more action in the years 1941-1944. I was away at a private school near Haslemere when Battle was bombed in February 1943, but my mother wrote to me about it. At the time none of us knew what a narrow escape the Abbey and the town had. A German bomber made a sneak raid, coming in through clouds, having cut out its engines, probably over the Channel, so that it would not be seen or heard until the last moment. Then it swooped down dropping a stick, as they were called, of six bombs. Four fell harmlessly in the valley between Caldbec Hill and Marley Lane, although they probably broke a few windows. One landed on the newsagent in the High Street, where today Martins newsagent is. It killed the shop keeper and his wife instantaneously. The other hit the base of the Abbey Gateway on the left as you enter the Abbey. It knocked out several base building blocks – their replacements are still a little paler than the originals. Fortunately the bomb was a dud. It concussed the Canadian sentry on duty at the Gateway but caused no other casualties. This was very lucky. No civilian in Battle knew that the Abbey was used to store an immense amount of ammunition which, if the bomb had gone off, would have destroyed the Gateway and much of the heart of Battle. We only learnt about this after the war. These sneak raids on the South East were quite frequent but killed few people although a primary school in Horsham was hit and, if I remember rightly, about 30 children were killed.

The area round my private school (Highfield at Liphook) was attacked in a sneak raid at night in 1943. We all had to leave our dormitories and go down to the ground floor. The raid was very noisy but did no harm.

Even less effective were the 'butterfly' bombs which were dropped in the middle of the war (1942-43).

I think they only killed about a dozen people in the whole country, although thousands must have been dropped. I was more frightened by them than by all the other attacks. I was frightened by the 'butterfly' bombs (so-called because they looked rather like large butterflies with

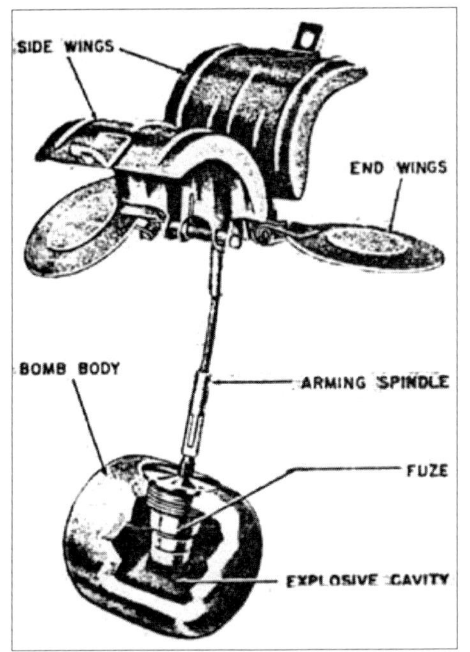

Left: Diagram of a butterfly bomb

Below: Doodlebug

wing shapes stuck on either side of what I think was a fuse). Their official name was 'anti-personnel bombs' but my father, who was a stickler for good, clear English, never used the term because he said that all bombs were 'anti-personnel'. They were frightening because they were scattered in the fields sometimes landing on bridle or foot paths but more often in cornfields. They lay there and blew up only if somebody or an animal trod on them. One of my father's and other doctors' duties was to sit by the edge of a cornfield when the harvest was being cut so that the harvester would have medical assistance to hand if one exploded. No doctor near Battle ever had to treat a harvester injured in such a way. Although the bombs were so ineffective, it was a very nasty feeling that, when going for a ride or a walk on a summer day, you could be mutilated or killed by just putting your foot in the wrong place.

The flying bombs, VIs or 'Doodle bugs' as they were usually called were more dangerous but we often enjoyed them! They were designed at Peenemunde on the Baltic coast of Germany and made mostly by slave workers of the Nazis (at Peenemunde these were mostly Frenchmen).

One or perhaps several of these men courageously smuggled this information out and the news reached London in time for the RAF to bomb Peenemunde, greatly delaying the deployment of the VIs, the official German name for these weapons. They were pilotless, powered by an engine which shot flaming exhaust from the tail, and stuffed full of high explosives. They made a loud, harsh noise. They began to arrive in Southern England a few days after D-Day on 6th June 1944. They were launched from North Eastern France and the Belgian coast RAF fighter planes tried to shoot them down into the Channel. Anti-aircraft guns lined up on the sea fronts of Hastings and other south coast towns tried to blow them up as they crossed the coast. If they survived this, the fighter planes tried to shoot them down into the woods to prevent them reaching London or other places with high density of population. This meant that a large number fell or blew up over the Battle District Council area.

I first saw a Doodlebug when travelling on the coastal railway after the end of the summer term at Highfield. I think the train was near Worthing.

I heard an ear-splitting noise and saw the flying bomb come in from the sea. I rushed to the other side of the train and saw it roaring on towards Greater London. Other Doodlebugs I saw or heard were all closer to home. They continued to arrive in large numbers until summer's end.

One day I was out riding accompanied by my two sisters in a pony trap on the road between Sedlescombe and Cripps Corner. A pursuing fighter plane, blazing away with its machine guns, blew the Doodlebug up when it was directly over us at a few hundred feet. The explosion was loud but the ponies, after one start, remained calm. Because there was so little traffic, the roads were much safer for riders than now.

Most of the Doodlebugs came during the day but one that came to Whatlington on a hot August night had a comic consequence. It landed near the Riccards Lane-Stream Lane cross-roads on the western side of the A21 at about 11.00 pm. I was in bed but the blast blew a mirror with a heavy wooden frame onto the bed, landing on my shins but not injuring me. All the lights failed. Quite a lot of plaster came down from the ceiling in the hall and dining room and a few windows were cracked and tiles blown off, but no structural damage was done. A Victorian brick cottage on the southern side of Stream Lane overlooking the cross-roads was nearer the explosion and my mother decided we should go to see if the people there were alright. In the dark I put on a coat hanging in a wall cupboard in the panelled room I used as a bedroom. My sisters, mother and I then walked the furlong or so to the cottage. The inhabitants were standing outside but quite unharmed, although the cottage had a crack running through its brick wall from top to bottom. We asked after each other in the neighbourly way being in the war together encouraged and then we returned to Hancox. As we left we were puzzled that our neighbours were suppressing laughter but when we reached home we discovered that the coat I had put on over my pyjamas was my brother's tail coat, a curious sartorial combination.

On another occasion in the same month a Doodlebug came down nearer the Royal Oak and closer still to Hancox in the heat of the day. A dozen or perhaps a score of people assembled near the Hancox drive entrance on the A21. My mother heard one man say: "A pity it didn't land on Hancox." My mother said: "Oh thank you very much." The man, embarrassed, said: "Oh no your ladyship of course I don't mean you" but with returning confidence "but we all know who we do mean". This was because the son-in-law of our tenant farmer at Hancox Farm had been one of Oswald Mosley's 'blackshirts' before the war and I think briefly imprisoned in 1940.

On another occasion my mother, sisters and I were in Hastings on the sea side of Warrior Square when five Doodlebugs came over. The anti-aircraft guns on the front (I think Bofors made in Sweden) blew them all up in a second or two as they neared the beach. Many of these coastal guns were manned (or I should say 'womanned') by ATS, as the women soldiers in the Army were called. Oddly I don't remember whether these ones were.

On one occasion earlier in the war Mrs. Whistler, Ralfe Whistler's mother who had served in the First World War as a driver and a canteen worker, seeing a young ATS lieutenant in Battle, invited her to Caldbec House for tea. Mrs. Whistler asked her name. The young officer said shyly: "Mary Churchill". She was Churchill's youngest child. They kept in touch and in 1970, just about Armistice Day, when I was in Paris with Jeremy Thorpe, the Liberal leader, as his private secretary, I met Mary Soames (*née* Churchill) at the British Embassy. Sir Christopher Soames was British Ambassador. Lady Soames spoke warmly of Mrs. Whistler.

Mrs Joan Whistler pre-war

I cannot end this account of the Doodlebugs without recalling three more things: one kindly but slightly comic, the other two sad but splendid. The first was that when the VIs had ceased to fall, the borough of Croydon was so grateful to the Battle Rural District Council area for absorbing so many Doodlebugs (about 2,000 I think), many of which might otherwise have fallen on Croydon, that it decided that any inhabitant of Battle RDC could have a free meal in Croydon. I do not think the gastronomic heights of Croydon rose very high after 5½ years of rationing and Croydon was hardly Soho or the West End at the best of times, but it was a kindly gesture.

The sad but splendid incidents were a little way from Battle but both concerned Doodlebugs that probably flew over the Battle District Council land. A flying bomb headed towards Benenden in Kent. A French pilot in the RAF intercepted it and tried to shoot it down. He ran out of ammunition but realised the VI would hit Benenden School which was being used as a military hospital (the girls had been evacuated, I think to the West Country in 1940). The pilot, who was of an aristocratic family, rammed the flying bomb and saved the hospital, He must have known he had no chance of survival. Fortunately this was witnessed by people on the ground. Fifty years later, in the presence of members of his family, a plaque recording his act of valour was unveiled in Benenden church.

The other story of heroism under the flying bomb attacks I heard soon after it occurred. Sadly, so far as I know it has no memorial. Many Italian prisoners of war arrived from 1942 mainly from North Africa. As only a few of the Fascist regiments and a few crack units of the regular Italian services really wanted to fight and so needed watching, most of the prisoners were employed as farm workers. There was a camp on the edge of Robertsbridge off the A21 which since the War has become a council house estate, but in 1942-45 housed a few hundred of these men. After Italy changed sides on 8th September 1943, Mussolini having been deposed six or seven weeks earlier, they were no longer prisoners but they could not be re-patriated until the War ended. Giovanni di Valentino aged 19 worked on a farm near Heathfield. In summer 1944 a flying bomb landed on the cow shed and set it ablaze. The farmer was inside attending to the cows. The Italian was outside and rushed into the cow shed to try to save the farmer. The roof collapsed and both men perished in the flames. Besides the heroism of the

Italian, this also speaks well of the local farmer. He must have behaved well to the Italian to inspire such devotion.

Daily Life 1939-45

The war pervaded every aspect of life. Food rationing got stricter from the end of 1939 and was very well organized after the formation of the Coalition Government in May 1940. Lord Woolton, a Conservative businessman, was an extremely efficient Minister of Food. He used to give talks on the BBC about what was available to be shared. The armed services and men, like miners doing heavy manual labour, were well fed even if their healthy diet must have been monotonous at times. Special care for women who were pregnant or who had small children to care for: they got extra rations. Concentrated orange juice and milk was provided free at schools and the children had much healthier food than many of them had had before the war. Consequently the nation became much healthier.

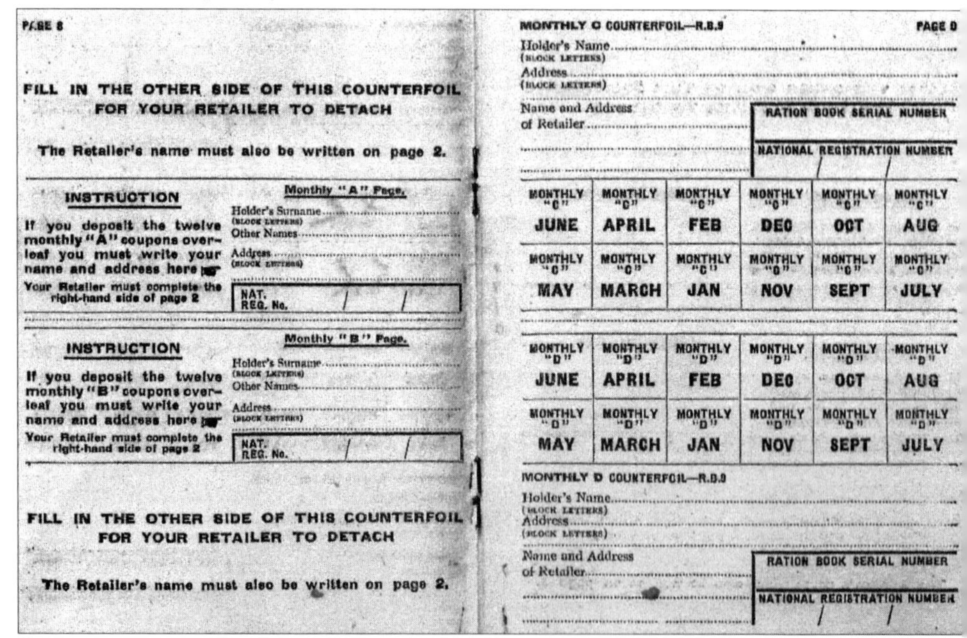
PAGE 8

FILL IN THE OTHER SIDE OF THIS COUNTERFOIL
FOR YOUR RETAILER TO DETACH

The Retailer's name must also be written on page 2.

INSTRUCTION

If you deposit the twelve monthly "A" coupons overleaf you must write your name and address here

Your Retailer must complete the right-hand side of page 2

Monthly "A" Page.
Holder's Surname (BLOCK LETTERS)
Other Names
Address (BLOCK LETTERS)
NAT. REG. No. / /

INSTRUCTION

If you deposit the twelve monthly "B" coupons overleaf you must write your name and address here

Your Retailer must complete the right-hand side of page 2

Monthly "B" Page.
Holder's Surname (BLOCK LETTERS)
Other Names
Address (BLOCK LETTERS)
NAT. REG. No. / /

FILL IN THE OTHER SIDE OF THIS COUNTERFOIL
FOR YOUR RETAILER TO DETACH

The Retailer's name must also be written on page 2.

MONTHLY C COUNTERFOIL—R.B.9 PAGE 9

Holder's Name (BLOCK LETTERS)
Address (BLOCK LETTERS)
Name and Address of Retailer

RATION BOOK SERIAL NUMBER

NATIONAL REGISTRATION NUMBER / /

MONTHLY "C" JUNE	MONTHLY "C" APRIL	MONTHLY "C" FEB	MONTHLY "C" DEC	MONTHLY "C" OCT	MONTHLY "C" AUG
MONTHLY "C" MAY	MONTHLY "C" MARCH	MONTHLY "C" JAN	MONTHLY "C" NOV	MONTHLY "C" SEPT	MONTHLY "C" JULY

MONTHLY "D" JUNE	MONTHLY "D" APRIL	MONTHLY "D" FEB	MONTHLY "D" DEC	MONTHLY "D" OCT	MONTHLY "D" AUG
MONTHLY "D" MAY	MONTHLY "D" MARCH	MONTHLY "D" JAN	MONTHLY "D" NOV	MONTHLY "D" SEPT	MONTHLY "D" JULY

MONTHLY D COUNTERFOIL—R.B.9

Holder's Name (BLOCK LETTERS)
Address (BLOCK LETTERS)
Name and Address of Retailer

RATION BOOK SERIAL NUMBER

NATIONAL REGISTRATION NUMBER / /

Ration book

However, if you were a bachelor bank clerk, say, you must have felt hungry. Although bread was never rationed during the War and nor were vegetables, nearly everything else was. For a long time the egg ration for the civilians who were not entitled to special rations, was one egg a week. Sugar was scarce. Butter was I think only 4 ounces a week. My sisters and I would cut a line in our butter to mark off Monday's butter, Tuesday's butter etc. for each day of the week. Very little fish was available. The Hastings fishermen, once the menace of invasion had gone, did bravely try to catch some, but of course they could not go far out in the Channel while the Germans held the French and Belgian coasts. I believe several Hastings fishermen were killed by air attacks while fishing.

Meat was very scarce but this was not so much of a problem in rural areas because there were pigeons, some game birds and huge numbers of rabbits to be shot or snared. We also used to shoot grey squirrels to eat. There was not much meat on a single squirrel but they tasted quite well. I had to eat rabbit so often that after rationing finally came to an end in the early 50s I never wanted to eat it again. I know rabbit can be delicious, but I have never been able to rid myself of this prejudice. Country dwellers could also vary their diet by gathering mushrooms and picking wild blackberries. We had a field, the Thirteen Acre was its rather dull name, at Hancox. It had never been ploughed and produced a wonderful number of delicious mushrooms. A single picker could easily fill two large garden baskets in a single morning in September. However the order came from the Ministry of Agriculture that it was to be ploughed up for wheat. While today it produces a few mushrooms, it has never recovered as a provider of this delicious food.

Special food we could get at Hancox were lampreys from a stream that runs through our fields. However there were only enough of them to provide a few meals. They are very tasty and I am not surprised that a medieval king died of a 'surfeit of lampreys.' We also, like many other people, kept hens for their eggs and their meat. I can't remember what share of the eggs we had to sell to the Ministry of Food, but I do remember that when we raised a large pig in the last year of the war, we were only allowed to keep half of it to eat ourselves. My sister Hilary kept a white nanny goat for its milk. Because of all these extras available to country dwellers, the black market was never as bad in and near Battle as it was in the cities and large towns. My parents regarded it as an absolute duty not to buy things on it. I think many people shared their view but by the end of the war the activities of the 'spivs' as the criminals who dealt in it were called, were less frowned on.

Clothes were rationed too. Looking back I realize what a boon jeans would have been, but they were unknown in England in 1939. As it was, mending and darning were very much the order of the day. Getting holes in woollen socks and sore heels were a minor bane of my boyhood. At Christmas the Ministry of Food added a few treats to our rations. A little more chocolate, some fresh oranges as opposed to concentrated juice. Mrs. Whistler's sister, who had married a very rich Canadian, used to send us and many other families she knew, extremely rich plum cakes densely packed with candied fruit. Less palatable were the powdered eggs sent from the United States as a form of food aid and tins and tins of spam, a sort of processed meat. Much margarine was made in this country. One called 'Stork' was regarded as the best. No wine or spirits were imported with one exception. After the Allies occupied most of the French colonies in the Mahgreb, Algerian red wine was allowed in and much talked about, people pretending it was better than it was. My parents, who drank little, did not buy it. Beer and ale continued to be produced throughout the war and were not rationed. Our small, about 7-acre, hop garden at Hancox produced its crop as it had done probably from the 16th century. My parents had to build a shelter of corrugated iron thickly covered with earth in a ditch next to the hop garden in case there was an air raid. I think it was only used once. The pickers were women, men past call-up age, and adolescents of Whatlington plus an occasional service man or woman on leave. My sisters and I did a little picking.

During the summer of 1943 a company of Canadian soldiers of perhaps 200 men came to Hancox and their commander asked if they could sleep in the house and garden as they were taking part in an exercise. The officers slept on the floor of the hall and dining room. Hancox garden has many walls and the following morning the Canadian captain asked if his men could scale over them. My parents agreed but when an officer tested a wall by shaking its top layer of bricks, it fell over so that particular exercise was abandoned.

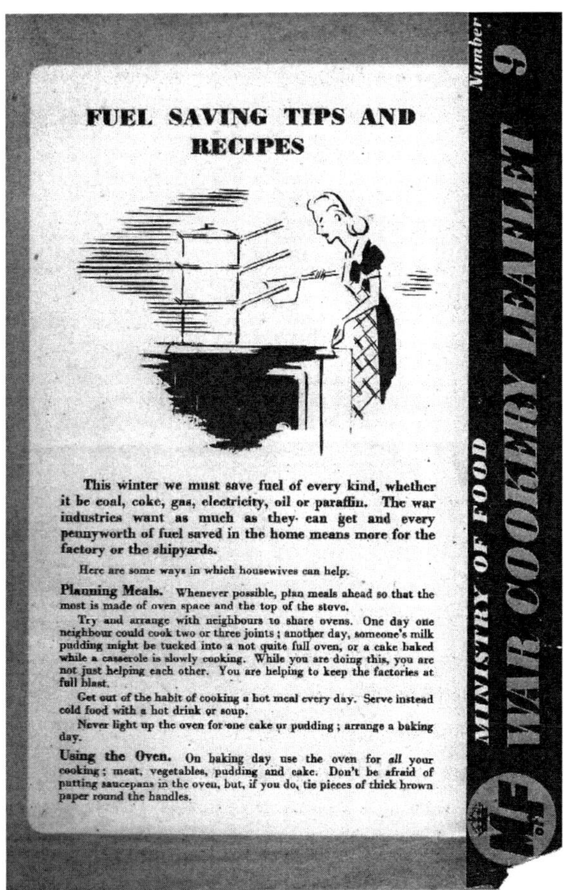

FUEL SAVING TIPS AND RECIPES

This winter we must save fuel of every kind, whether it be coal, coke, gas, electricity, oil or paraffin. The war industries want as much as they can get and every pennyworth of fuel saved in the home means more for the factory or the shipyards.

Here are some ways in which housewives can help.

Planning Meals. Whenever possible, plan meals ahead so that the most is made of oven space and the top of the stove.

Try and arrange with neighbours to share ovens. One day one neighbour could cook two or three joints ; another day, someone's milk pudding might be tucked into a not quite full oven, or a cake baked while a casserole is slowly cooking. While you are doing this, you are not just helping each other. You are helping to keep the factories at full blast.

Get out of the habit of cooking a hot meal every day. Serve instead cold food with a hot drink or soup.

Never light up the oven for one cake or pudding ; arrange a baking day.

Using the Oven. On baking day use the oven for *all* your cooking ; meat, vegetables, pudding and cake. Don't be afraid of putting saucepans in the oven, but, if you do, tie pieces of thick brown paper round the handles.

MINISTRY OF FOOD

WAR COOKERY LEAFLET

Number 9

Fuel saving promotional leaflet

Other effects of the war that I can remember as features of local life were that the deer escaped from the few deer parks in the Battle area.

Consequently, we have seen many more deer in the woods than probably since the Middle Ages. The taboo on shooting foxes so that they could be hunted broke down. My brother stalked and shot one in the Savernack field at Hancox on the September evening of the day before I first went to board at Highfield. I accompanied him and felt elated by his skill.

The most absurd restriction I can remember was connected with fox hunting. Somebody in the bureaucracy supposed that Germans would come ashore as fox hunters. How they were meant to bring their horses over in motor torpedo boats or submarines was not clear. They would have been the only vessels in the German navy small enough to have approached the coast un-detected. However this non-existent peril was taken quite seriously by some fool in Whitehall and hunts were not allowed to meet less than five miles from the coast! I started hunting in September 1943 when on holiday from school. Oddly I don't remember the restriction being ridiculed but it was I think dropped by 1944.

We all had to carry identity cards. Anybody in an official position could challenge people to produce them. Occasionally check points would be set up and everybody passing it was checked. I remember my younger sister Meriel, who took pleasure in teasing adults and was six or seven at the time, going round the policemen and one man not in uniform who were manning a check point at Lewes station, murmuring in a teasing voice: 'I'm not a spy.'

One of the good things about the war after Churchill took over, was that people were encouraged to make suggestions about how the efficiency of the war effort could be improved. I am sure that this led to many absurdities (I heard that somebody suggested that cormorants should be trained to fly to Essen in the Ruhr to pick the mortar out of the tall chimneys of the Krupps armament factories so that they would crash onto the works so seriously impairing the German war effort). But it did mean we felt that we were 'all in it together' to use a term less happily invoked in recent times. It led, for example, to the piling up in 1940 on village greens and town squares of old pots and pans, broken down bicycles and iron railings so that they could be melted down and turned into war planes. The village green in Whatlington had a fine heap. My father rode a wobbly and decayed Edwardian bicycle to it. We were not patriotic enough to sacrifice the Penny Farthing we still have in the Hancox garage. After the war, it emerged that very little of all this scrap metal was turned into planes but at the time it gave a sense of solidarity with the RAF to civilians.

My elder sister and I used to ride ponies to woods where many foxgloves grew to gather them for their digitalis which was good for the hearts of people bombed or shell shocked. Sometimes my sister would bring a first aid kit provided by the Girl Guides and practice on me as a war casualty.

Entertainment in the war was mainly provided by the cinema which played a huge part. Besides the Senlac cinema in Battle, there were no less than eight cinemas in Hastings. They were: the Gaiety, the De Luxe (both old music halls and fairly large), the Ritz (large), the Plaza (small), the Elite (small), the Kinema (small), the Roxy (small), and the Regal (enormous). The Gaiety is the only survivor – now called the ABC. Both the Elite in Warrior Square and the Plaza near to where W.H. Smith is today were bombed. The damage at the Elite was slight and no one was hurt but the Plaza was demolished and caused the greatest loss of life of any bomb that fell on Hastings. Thirteen people were killed. The films shown were often about the war, exalting the armed services as in 'In Which We Serve' for the Royal Navy, 'The First of the Few' for the designer of the Spitfire, 'The Way Ahead' for the Army, 'People like Us' and 'The Tawny Pippit' for the war effort in general, and 'The Gentle Sex' for the Women's Services.

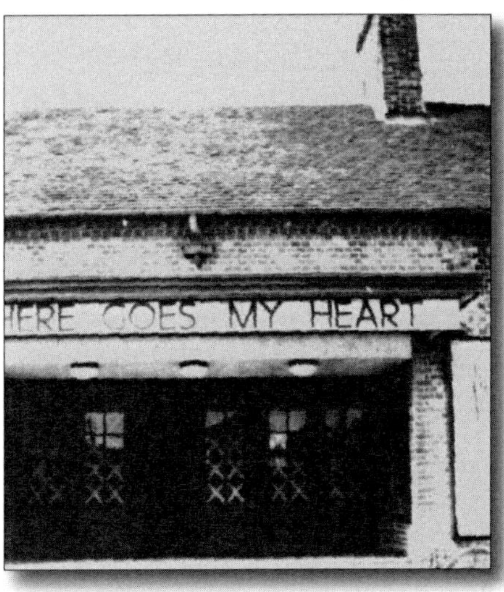

The front of the Senlac Cinema, now Burstow & Hewett, showing the wartime criss-cross strips on the glass panes in the doors

There were also documentaries like 'Desert Victory' about El

Alamein which were full length. Every programme included news reels which showed scenes from the fronts. Also the King and Queen making morale-raising visits and the meetings of Allied leaders. The first film I saw in the war in the Autumn of 1939 was 'The Lion Has Wings' about the RAF, and the last before VE Day was 'Western Approaches' about the North Atlantic convoys. That was in April 1945. At some point the programme was interrupted and the manager of the Regal Cinema took the stage. It could seat nearly 2,000 people in its block overlooking Warrior Square station and nearly every seat was taken that afternoon. The manager told us that President Roosevelt had died. There were gasps from the audience. By then he meant much to the British public.

The grimmest war films were often about the Resistance movements in Nazi-occupied countries. Comparing them with films made in countries which were, or had been, occupied by the Nazis (mainly French and Italian), I am struck by the naiveté of the British and even more of the American films. But they did have the merit of reminding us of the courage of the resistance fighters and of the fact that we had many friends across the Channel. This was also helped by a BBC programme on Sunday evenings when the national anthems of all the Allies were played. My memories of the BBC during the war are entirely positive. The BBC war correspondents who went straight into battles gave exciting commentaries of the actual fighting. I remember as especially vivid the commentary on General de Gaulle's walk from the Arc de Triomphe down the Champs Elysees to Notre Dame. French Nazis in Notre Dame tried to assassinate him and the BBC correspondent lay down to describe the scene. When the rising of the Parisians began a week before this, I remember being moved to tears when the BBC, having announced the news, played the Marseillaise.

I am sad that I heard few of Churchill's great speeches when they were first broadcast. This was probably because they were often broadcast after my bedtime but perhaps also because my parents did not want me to be alarmed by his tones of defiance when the defeat and conquest of this country seemed quite likely. I do however vividly remember hearing Churchill speak to a joint meeting of the two Houses of Congress in January

1941 thanking them for passing the Lend Lease Act which provided the British government with credit to buy American weapons and other essentials. The USA was still neutral then and so was the Soviet Union but Churchill was determined to try to draw the Americans into the war and eager too to encourage the British to feel that a great power was on their side, if not yet fighting. Hitler, later in 1941, solved that problem by invading the Soviet Union on 24th June and declaring war on the United States four days after Pearl Harbour on 11th December.

Occasionally we would go to Fairlight because of its beauty and because it was both comforting and a little sinister – a combination children like – to look out over the Channel towards the enemy. On a clear day you can see the French coast from Fairlight. We were there on one such day and I remember the eerie thrill it gave me to realize the enemy was so close.

I had a thrill a little similar in June 1943 when staying with my mother in my cousin Matthew Pryor's house in Bayswater. I was returning to school after several illnesses and I think my mother felt I needed a treat. I think that was the time when my mother took me to the National Gallery to see the one picture allowed out of the Welsh caves where the collection had been hidden to be safe from bombing at the beginning of the war. It would be exhibited for a month and then replaced by another great picture from the collection. When I went, it was Renoir's '*Les Parapluies*'. On the same visit I was 'polyphoto'd', then much in vogue as film for home cameras was un-obtainable. We went to see the film 'The Lady Vanishes' much enjoyed but it was at supper that I got my thrill. Matthew Pryor was an army officer working in intelligence, based in London. That evening he presented to his delightful Anglo-Irish wife Barbara, to my mother and me, a Camembert cheese given to him by one of those he worked with. It was in very good condition, fresh from Nazi-occupied Normandy.

A great hoax and a liberation

My brother Norman was called up in the autumn of 1942 and commissioned into the Royal Artillery in 1943. He was soon being trained as a Mountain Gunner in the Cairngorms. The Mountain Gunners were the last regiment in the British Army in which the officers were mounted. The guns were dismantled and carried by mules. I think eight, but perhaps ten batteries were trained in the Highlands. In February 1944 my brother had his embarkation leave. This was the leave all soldiers had before they were sent on active service in a theatre of war. My sister Hilary and I were allowed home from our boarding schools for its duration. He told his family a little of his training and wore the insignia of the Mountain Gunners. Being a great lover of nature and of wild places he had enjoyed his training whatever its hardships which, in the winter at least, must have been considerable. He returned to duty and continued to exchange letters with his family.

In mid-October we got his first letter from a theatre of war. It was from the Netherlands where he had taken part in the landings on Walcheren! What transpired was that he had been transferred to the Airborne Artillery. He was actually on the tarmac waiting to take off when the order came to send no more men to Arnhem where, in spite of the courage of the Paratroop Regiment and the courageous assistance of the Dutch civilians, the Germans (superior in numbers and weapons) overwhelmed them. My brother had transferred to the Airborne Artillery as part of a brilliant hoax which saved many Allied lives. Hitler was convinced that the Allies would land in Norway and the Allied High Command encouraged him in this delusion so that he kept several crack German

Norman Moore 1944

divisions in Norway rather than sending them to the Low Countries and France where they would have taken part in resisting the Allied landings in Normandy.

Six batteries of Mountain Gunners did serve as such in Burma, Italy and Greece, but the others became Airborne Artillery although my brother reached Walcheren by land. Canadians and Poles took part in this operation as well as British troops, some of them landing from the sea. My brother's battery was the first Allied unit into a small Dutch town called Udenhout. He became friends with the Dutch family on whom he was billeted, where he left his chocolate ration for the children for St Nicholas's Day. The family kept in touch and Norman was welcomed in the town by its *Burgameister* (Mayor) fifty years after its liberation. The families exchanged letters and visits until Norman's death in 2015.

In December 1944 the Germans nearly broke through the American lines in the Ardennes, but the Americans fought back very bravely and defeated the last major offensive of the German army in the War. To help their stand, British troops moved into some of the Americans' positions to the North just over the Belgian border in Germany and in Belgium, so that American troops could reinforce their compatriots in the Ardennes. My brother's battery was part of this deployment. He was in command of an observation post in No Man's Land just after Christmas. On 27th December the Second in Command of the battery joined him and the ten men of the battery in the observation post. Thirty infantry guarded the Gunners. On the morning of the 28th the Germans made an attack of battalion strength in thick mist. They took the British by surprise and wiped out the infantry in their 'fox holes', as the individual entrenchments were called. The Gunners hoped the Germans would not spot them and hid in the cellar of the house they had used as an observation post Unfortunately they had not had time to dismantle the wireless aerials they had been using to report to the battery's headquarters. The Germans dropped a grenade into the cellar. Amazingly, although all twelve of the British were wounded, none were killed. One of the Gunners died of wounds later. Norman's wounds were shrapnel wounds mainly in his right knee. The Second in Command of the battery, being the Senior Officer (he was a major, my brother only a Lieutenant) had to decide what to do. He rightly surrendered.

At first my brother was well treated. He was taken to a German field hospital for about ten days. A dying SS man in the next bed insisted on giving him chocolate. Suddenly one morning Norman was taken from the hospital and literally thrown into an open cattle truck on a railway. After a very cold journey he arrived at a prisoner-of-war camp near a town called Hemer in the Ruhr. It held about 30,000 men, two thirds of them Russians, with about 3,000 Poles, 3,000 French and the rest a mixture of nationalities. There was only one other British officer who sadly died soon after the camp's liberation. There were about a dozen Americans and several Canadians. The conditions in the camp were deplorable. The prisoners from the Western Countries and the Poles, being in countries that adhered to the Geneva Convention on the treatment of prisoners of war, were better treated than the Russians because the Soviet Union had not signed the Geneva Convention. The Nazis regarded them as sub-human '*untermenschen*'. Rations for the Western soldiers were half a litre of mangle wurzel soup a day and a loaf of black bread a week. The Russians got the soup but the loaf was divided between 48 men! While the Germans had to subsist on very dull food, they had plenty of it. The housewives returning from the market used often to throw potatoes and scraps over the wire. Sometimes this may have been an act of mercy but they often enjoyed watching the Russians fighting over the food. Every morning there were dead Russians who, under cover of darkness, had crawled to the wire to try to pick grass and weeds beyond the wire to eat.

Norman lost four stone in the three months he was in the camp. He got on very well with the other officers. (Under the Geneva Convention officers and non-commissioned ranks were always held in separated quarters). On his 22nd birthday (24th February) the Polish officers clubbed together and gave him a loaf of black bread from their rations. There were very scanty medical supplies. Toilet paper had to be boiled and used as dressings. The Serbian Army doctor, who was the only doctor among the officers, had often to sit down from weakness in the middle of operations. He was assisted by French medical orderlies. Norman remembered that the Serb sometimes had to perform amputations without anaesthetics because there were none.

Soon after Hitler's birthday (20th April) which some Germans after the War said was the last day when they believed they might somehow win the War, American tanks smashed through the barbed wire of the camp at Hemer and the Germans fled or surrendered. The Russians succeeded in lynching or shooting quite a number of Germans, many of whom had been guilty of kicking or beating the Russians. The Western officers, together with the Poles, armed themselves and imprisoned about twelve hundred Germans in a large secondary school to protect them. My brother took pleasure in throwing flower pots at a painting of Hitler patting a young girl on the head. American infantry and army medical teams soon arrived. My brother was flown to an American hospital at Rheims where about twelve days later the German High Command formally surrendered to the Supreme Allied Commander, General Eisenhower. After a day or two in the American hospital Norman was flown to a British hospital at Leeds. He was in an American Dakota, the trusted work horse transport plane of the Western Allies. It flew low and, looking out of a window, my brother realized it was passing over Hancox. (The house and land is quite easily recognizable from the air because of the configuration of the fields and, if low enough, the garden walls. I have recognized it several times flying to Gatwick.) He said to the American Red Cross sergeant: "That's my home down there."

"Gee bud" said the American, "do you want a parachute!"

All this, from the time when he was taken prisoner to his journey home, we only learnt later. His last letter to us before he was captured was an account of how a Christmas dinner was served with, as was the British Army's custom, the officers waiting on the men. We had been told he was missing on 2nd January. About three weeks later we had a Red Cross form saying he was a prisoner. We did not get a letter from him until some weeks later. It told us only of his friendship with the Allied officers. The German censors would not have allowed news of the dreadful conditions out. I think we only got one letter. The news of his liberation reached my parents on their 23rd wedding anniversary, the 26th April. My mother went to Leeds to bring him home by train. On 2nd May they reached Battle. My father drove my sisters and I in his battered old Austin to bring him home to Hancox. We had fixed Union Jacks to the front mudguards. As we came back from the station my sisters and I leaned out of the windows shouting: "Liberated prisoner – hurrah!"

After the War in Europe ended my brother gave evidence to the War Crimes Commission about the camp in Hemer. Investigators went there. The local inhabitants denied all knowledge of the camp. No prosecutions were made.

There were celebrations all over the country on VE Day 8th May. We had a bonfire behind the Royal Oak at Whatlington. A few days later the service men and women from Whatlington were given a supper at the Village Hall. I remember the Chairman of the Parish Council apologized to Norman privately because at the supper he had been placed next to a service woman (who may have been a Land Girl) who had used the opportunity of working alongside men to conduct more than several amorous encounters.

In mid-May a parade was held in Battle of all the Civilian Services who had been part of the local War effort. My father took part, marching with the St John's Ambulance Brigade, the Women's Voluntary Services, the Police, the Air Raid Wardens, the Land Army women. I do not remember whether there were representatives of the Home Guard which had been stood down in 1944. I remember my mother telling me of the courage of Mrs Hayes who lived at Battle Mill. She attended the parade as a spectator although her son John, who was a Lieutenant in the airborne forces, had been killed only a few days before the surrender of the German High Command. He was in a plane shot down about the same time as my brother was liberated.

On 21st July there was a Victory Fête at Hancox. There were pony rides, sports like sack and egg and spoon races for the children which were run on the tennis lawn which by then was rough because there had been no petrol for the lawn mower for nearly six years. There was a tea in the dining room and I think on some outside tables as well. Then there was an entertainment in the drawing room which was packed out. There was a conjuror and his wife who sang, did good mimicry and got my father, who loathed dancing, to perform the Hokey Cokey. At the end we all sang Rule Britannia.

On 26th July we listened to the news of the General Election. People in Great Britain had voted on 5th July but it took until 26th to get all the ballot boxes back from the theatres of war, the warships and the British bases in many parts of the world. My sister Hilary was aghast at the defeat of the Tories (in later life she was a staunch Liberal). Her school at St Mary's Calne was a good one but many of its pupils came from very Conservative homes. My parents and I think my brother had all voted Liberal. I put on my father's straw hat 'at a jaunty angle' as Hilary described in her diary, in celebration of Labour's victory. My parents and Norman, besides their vote in the Rye division which included Battle and Whatlington, had a vote for a university seat, my mother for Oxford and the men for Cambridge. The Labour Government legislated to abolish the University seats in 1948.

On 6th August we went to Michelham Priory to enjoy its beauty and tranquillity. When we got home we turned on the wireless and learned of the atom bomb being dropped on Hiroshima. We all felt that it was right to end the War by using the atom bomb as quickly as possible as did the great majority of people, although some changed their minds when the horror of radio-active injuries was reported.

On the morning of 15th August I heard the news on the BBC of Japan's surrender. I rushed to my sister Meriel's bedroom where she was still in bed. She burst into tears because Norman had been re-called to his regiment three days before and so could not light the Whatlington bonfire which he had been invited to do. It went ahead behind the Royal Oak where there was much celebration and I swigged my first gin. Afterwards I walked into Battle on a lovely summer night. The bonfire on the Green before the Abbey was still smouldering at three in the morning with a few people standing round.

That was the end of the War but for many people in the Battle area I think the greatest celebration came on Guy Fawkes Day, 5th November. Because of the black-out there had been no celebration of Guy Fawkes Day since 1938. It had for generations been celebrated with great vigour in every village in East Sussex. Battle's celebration was second only to Lewes, as is the case to this day, in size and enthusiasm. Mrs. Whistler kindly put me up at Caldbec House so I could enjoy the whole event. There was a great sense of solidarity that evening. Nearly everybody joined in. The generations, the classes, the sexes all marched and intermingled with enthusiasm. I found myself marching next to a groom called Mr Wren. Suitably with such a name, he was a very small man. He was wearing his jodhpurs and gaiters just as he had when giving me riding lessons in Battle Abbey Park in the Spring of 1939. There was a happy combination of nostalgia for the pleasures of times past, of a bit of glory at having endured and been on the winning side and even on the front line, in a great struggle with evil and of the near universal desire to build a better country. At 14 I was old enough to sense this."

Richard Moore
Battle
November 2018

THE STORY OF BATTLE'S REX PEARSON

Based on his 1939-45 diaries

Rex on leave, 1939

A life most ordinary

Nothing in Rex's civilian life at Battle could have prepared him for his wartime experiences. Describing his life in 1939 he says:

> "A typical week would be to work from 8 am to 5.30 pm Monday to Friday and in the evenings visit each others' houses, playing cards or snooker, chasing after girls, or earlier on enjoying the scout troop activities. On Saturday it was work to 12.30 or 1.00pm, going home for

> dinner and change for the 2.30 kick off for the local football eleven. Then home for a wash and a bath if the solid fuel boiler in the corner of the bathroom was going, baling the water from it into the bath. Then tea and change and off to a local dance or by 'chara' to another town or village dance, and so to bed. Without a car in the non-existent car park, it might well mean a 3-mile plus walk to see a girl home if you were that keen. On Sunday it was off with the gang, in a car – fortunately borrowed by a friend from his father – to roller skating at an open air swimming pool."

With his friends, Rex joined the Royal Engineers in August 1939.

The Nazi threat

Rex and his friends settle down to training at Eastbourne, memorable for physical training done while wearing hobnail boots. There was special training in bridge-moving for a visit by George VI, but "The day the King came, we just saw him from a distance, a three second glance and away again." However, the training did not divert the men from being focused on the Nazi threat:

> "The German machine was gearing up for all our country bashing. "We are the greatest...we are the world masters to be" were prevalent doctrines. They saw themselves as breeding pure pedigree stock, and party members virtually guaranteeing their offsprings' indoctrination from birth. Under the Nazi flag and doctrine held together by a real display of unity in the party, were the brown shirts. They were backed up by the military power displayed by the SS; and there were the Hitler Youth organisations, uniformed. Everything was ensured by the more potent force of everyone watching and reporting others, which included children reporting parents and there was also the undisplayed force, the Gestapo (secret police)."

Arrival in France: and a nasty surprise

After seven months' training in Gravesend, the Royal Engineers arrived in Le Havre in early April 1940, having successfully dodged the U-boats. To begin with, life was good: 'We spent our evenings in the villages around, very nice people … we had cheese from farmhouses, bacon and eggs and real country cider of which some of us occasionally had too much.' The company then moved south to Doullens (below), a town like Hastings but they found it deserted.

Doullens today

> "The whole place was empty apart from odd dogs and cats, nothing, you could hear the silence. This was very eerie and almost supernatural. The houses were left with crockery and cutlery on the tables, beds made or unmade. In the pubs, glasses were still on the tables and the bar. The population had left in a hurry with anything they could transport on their backs or in carts, but it seemed more as if a magic wand had been waved and all had been plucked up by one huge hand."

Ordered to collect a lorry-full of anti tank mines, Rex and a small detachment set off to the centre of Doullens at crack of dawn, rightly concerned, as it turned out, at being separated from the rest of the Company, their only communications being two despatch riders on motorcycles, conveying their orders. Having stocked up, to their amazement, at a Salvation Army canteen, Rex and his men were "sitting around munching sweets and having a smoke, when we had rather a nasty shock, because the announcer on the wireless said that German armour was sweeping through and were expected to take Doullens in a couple of hours. The information was not accepted immediately. Then we woke up to the fact that we were sitting in the square of Doullens. This was the first we had heard that the war had got onto our heels. We received an order to move on and were quite pleased to get cracking."

Suddenly Rex and the 12 men with him were pitched into the horror of chaotic evacuation in the face of the German forces, with Stuka bombers strafing the roads, jam packed with "this stupefied, scared, brave mass of humanity .... The problem was no one knew where the front was. The armoured columns of Germans heading acress country towards the coast meant that the so-called front could be in front of you, then when you travelled 20 miles in the opposite direction, it was there as well.At one point we were told by the Military police that we were surrounded, we kept going and must have found a gap. When the roads were impassable we took to the fields, then back to the road or lane when it was seen to be clearer."

Capture

Following further encounters with German tanks, Rex's group briefly rejoined the Company before being separated again, going from Doullens in the opposite direction to Boulogne, where the rest of the Company eventually embarked for England. All seemed well to begin with, until Rex and his truck came to a tunnel, 11pm 20th May 1940. Suddenly 'all hell was let loose. Our truck stopped dead, the road was blocked. There were tracer bullets criss-crossing through and over the truck. Suddenly there were Jerrys with automatic weapons. We really did suddenly realise that war was around us and that we were in the middle of it. We were told in English to get out of the truck : we did just that and lined up. The Jerrys threatened to shoot us, offering a last smoke if we wanted one, and took our rifles and broke them in half. They were tall, had shorn heads, very confident and over-disciplined.'

The march to Poland

Rex's group of about 20 was soon joined by many others – French, Belgians, and Moroccans – forming into a large column. This was the start of a three week march. There was no food and water had to be scrounged when it rained. A truck at the front and the rear had a mounted machine gun and a German officer rode around on horseback, supervising. Rex was not to know it, but he was one of some 30,000 PoWs captured in this operation. Rex adopted the 'mucker' principle, in which a friend looks out for you: "you pooled ideas, clothes, when one was lying down keeping the spot, the other was out trying to find something to eat or drink."

The column reached the Siegfried Line where the German soldiers, in confident mood, taunted Rex and his group about being in England soon, what was the food like in England and so on. Rex resumes the narrative about what happened when they reached the Luxembourg border:

> "On reaching the Luxembourg border we were stopped and told we were going by train. This sounded good. What in fact happened was that cattle trucks arrived and sixty men were locked into each. After a long wait we chugged slowly on our way. Every hour things got a little worse: we were holding each other up because of the numbers. Two days and three nights passed, including a stop in the Berlin suburbs when porters and civilians were using water but our requests for a drink were ignored. At last in a pretty poor state and in a pretty stinky mess state at that, we reached somewhere and fell out into a station in the wilds. Some didn't make it and others were too bad to get out on their own. We then marched and staggered two or three miles, seeing absolutely nothing, and this brought us to a medieval fort. We realised afterwards that this was in fact in the Polish corridor and that it was a Polish Army fort."

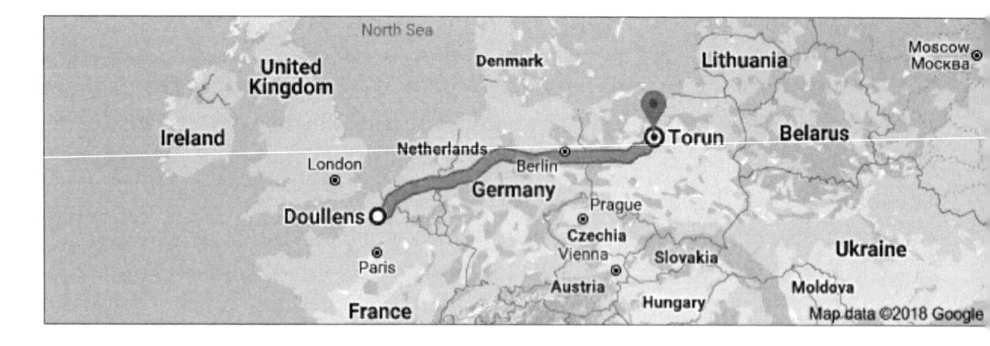

Doullens to Torun POW camp: 1,329 km.

(Base Map © Google2018)

Prisoner of War in Poland

They had reached Torun PoW camp Stalag XXA Fort 11, which was to be their base until the end of 1944: a forbidding place with steel bridge, empty moat and steel portcullis.

Stalag XXA Fort 11

For Rex the next four and a half years were to be spent in several PoW camps at or in the vicinity of, Torun. The PoWs worked on a variety of construction projects: clearing forests, installing sewerage schemes, building houses and schools. We know now that they were a small part of the *lebensraum* project to provide new living areas for Germans in a greater Germany. This is Rex's map:

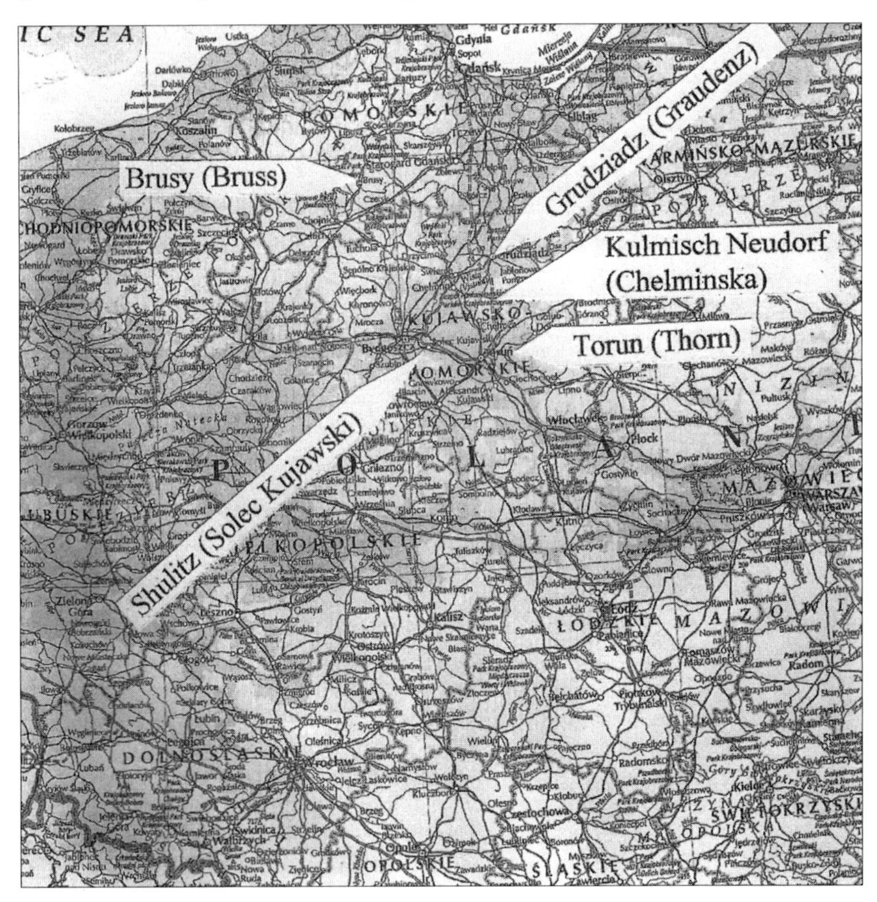

POW camps in Poland in which Rex Pearson was imprisoned

Whether deliberate or not, the moving between camps damaged morale, as Rex recalls: "one of the gruelling experiences was the movement away from the friendships formed, and having to start all over again with completely new men." After about 10 months, it was evident that PoW life was affecting men in different ways: "...there was now some semblance of law and order. Wherever you are there are 'wide boys' who were doing alright for themselves, and others, the losers still wandering around picking up the crumbs. The improvement in 10 months was remarkable but there were still some who could not make the effort after the truck travel and had to be forcibly cleaned up and jarred into acceptance of a new life."

For Rex's loved ones at home, morale was an issue as well: he was posted as missing and there was no news until August when the following Red Cross card arrived, incorrectly stating the location of the camp as Germany not Poland:

Ref. N° (RECEIVED 1ST JULY) 242 b-bis

RBO 1525 Geneva, 17th June '40

Dear Madam, (Sir)

We beg to inform you that we have received a card dated 9th June '40 from the STALAG XX A(3) Germany advising us that PEARSON REX SAPPER R.E. born 19. 2. 1921 is interned in that camp.

From now on you can send letters to the above mentioned prisoner of war to the address given, adding the following : " Kriegsgefangenenpost " (prisoners of war post) and " Gebührenfrei " (free of postal charges).

is well

Yours faithfully.
Comité International de la Croix Rouge
Agence centrale des prisonniers de guerre
GENÈVE

News that Rex Pearson has been found

It was ten months until the first family letters began arriving at Torun via the Red Cross. These and the Red Cross parcels – whose frequency gradually improved – were a vital part of prisoner morale and, in the case of the parcels, their diet. A thin soup and a piece of black bread was the daily ration at Torun; potatoes had to be stolen or bartered, and usually eaten raw. At other camps, mashed potato and stewed plums were on offer. Clogs and 'sweat squares' substituted for shoes and socks. Every day was a struggle for survival. Rex became ill due to the insufficient food and for a while had to be moved from heavy labouring duties. Lice were prevalent and due to the primitive arrangements, dysentery was common.

Rex had some photographs of camp social activities but behind the façade, some were organised for Nazi propaganda purposes. This one from Schulitz camp 1941 (Rex is arrowed) was probably authentic:

Schulitz PoW camp 1941

But the one below, taken at Graudenz camp circa 1943, showing some kind of improvised band, was probably not. From Rex's account, the rumour mill and the battle with Nazi propaganda was always present: "Rumours boosted our spirits one moment, dashed them the next." Lack of certainty about how long an Allied victory would take took its toll. The remoteness of the camps made escape futile and inhibited contact with the outside world. For all that Rex noticed some escape activity, mainly men he did not know arriving and leaving with new clothes, presumably on some kind of camp-to-camp escape route.

Nazi-organised postcard of PoWs apparently enjoying themselves

Communications with family at home could only happen through the *Kriegsgefangenpost*, a German-censored postal service for PoWs. Cards took months, were heavily stamped by the Nazi censor, and were not received or sent at all if the geographical location of the camp, other than its number, was mentioned. Rex noticed that as the war went on, the activities of the Gestapo became more evident, with more searches for the prisoners, and penalties for the soldiers if they did not sing in praise of Hitler loudly enough, or were caught giving an army salute instead of the Nazi one.

The Long March to Germany

In the face of the advancing Russians, the long march to Germany for Rex and the other PoWs began in late December 1944. The Germans did this on the basis that the PoWs could be bartered or be cannon fodder. "Next day we carried on marching again and were joined with more and more PoWs. In a matter of two or three weeks we were thousands on the march. If you stopped, you stood a good chance of being shot. We had some young and mean guards but gradually they were replaced by older ones. ...Our goods and chattels had to be gradually thrown away as we got too weak to carry them. There wasn't any food or water and we were using the snow to keep our mouths moist."

Rex continues: "We marched and marched. We had to walk with eyes half closed against the snow light and more or less subconscious at times. We were sleeping in commandeered barns. We were marching more or less by will power, our minds were on home and our eyes continuously looking for food and water." When they got to a barn for the night "the whole thing was a swirling mass of starving men all over the barn ... A number of men, mostly older ones, dropped out during the march. Some were looked after, others just died, frostbite was a real menace too." Lice were a problem again as it was now February 1945 and nobody had taken their clothes off for over two months. As they marched deeper into Germany and April came, the dynamics of the march changed: the column changed into smaller groups. The guards' food supply ceased so they were now looking for food in the same way as the prisoners and were disciplined by the SS for not keeping order. Strafing was frequent, but by Allied planes, not Stukas. Rex joined a small splinter group when the march reached a village south of Hamburg.

Rescue

At this point, 18 April 1945, the 11th Armoured Division arrived and Rex had been rescued: "British tanks capture hospital and carry on towards Luneburg. 400 of us here, half dead with fatigue. Dozen or so walk off, find farm and two cottages all empty. Tanks come and went straight through both cottages. We had tea and biscuits, dared not eat anything else, bags of smokes, we cried openly, couldn't speak properly for hours. God what a day." Rex was flown to a hospital near Brussels by 21 April and had his first hot bath for five years: "I do not have the novelist's art to describe this usually normal event, this was indeed the event of a lifetime." Clean sheets and pyjamas are 'heaven personified'. Rex weighs in at 7stone 2lb, three and a half stone underweight.

On 23 April 1945 Rex flies home, wangling his way into the Dakota (probably C47, interior pictured below) cockpit and persuading the pilot to divert a little over Hastings and Battle on the way to a military airport near Swindon.

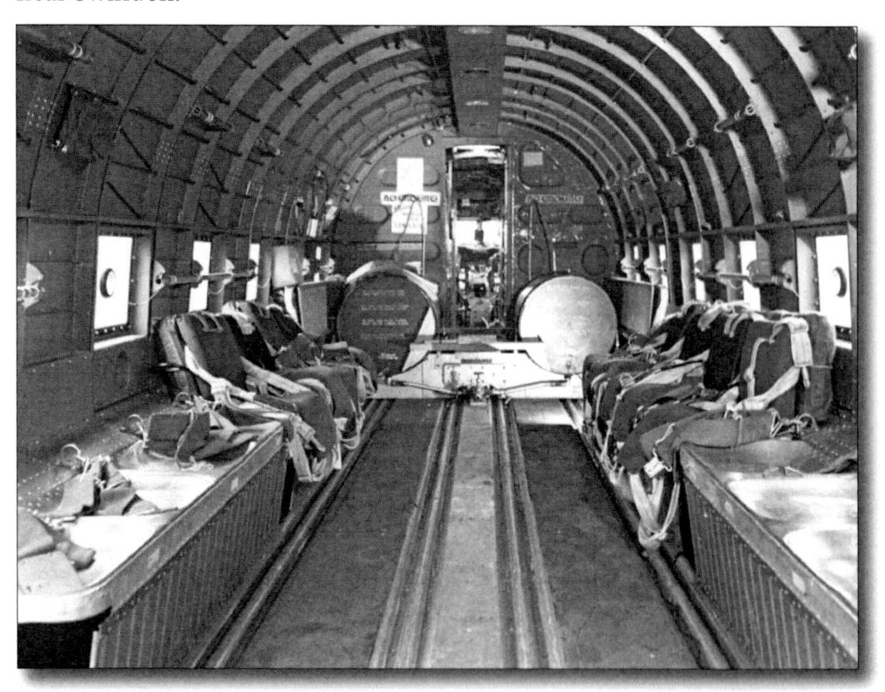

C47 and home

But before his departure, there was a jarring note for Rex, perhaps foretelling of the desire for social change which swept Attlee to power a couple of months later: "In a marquee, dishing out books and comforts, were uniformed women, 25-30 years. It came as an unpleasant shock to me that despite six years of upset of all known normalities, this lot were acting like 1920s/30s debutantes, toffee-nosed, looking through you as if you were invisible, talking among themselves and ignoring us, and talking in the same old plum-in-the-mouth style. I felt disappointed that there had not been any levelling whatsoever."

After medical checks Rex was released to go home to fiancée Ruth Wood in Battle on 28 April 1945. What happened then is told in 'Ruth's Story', which follows.

THE STORY OF RUTH PEARSON

While Rex Pearson was struggling to stay alive as a PoW in Poland and on the dreadful journey back, Ruth Wood his fiancée was surviving in her own way back home in England. This is an account of the story she told – as Ruth Pearson – over seventy years later, to family and friends on 14th May 2018 at Battle Museum.

Lovers parted

The forced separation of hundreds of thousands of British couples had a huge impact on national demography and Ruth and Rex were no exceptions. Ruth was 16 when she met Rex, three years older, in 1940, in her home town of Gravesend. He had been in the Territorial Reserve before the war and volunteered in 1939. A Battle man, Rex would doubtless never have met Ruth were it not for war duties taking him to Gravesend. In Ruth's words, when he joined up, Rex was 'a handsome, upright, dapper fellow...a lovely man.' They had hardly got to know each other before Rex went to serve in France and they were not to see each other, as happened for millions of lovers, until 1945. But they confirmed their love by getting engaged by proxy: Rex's sister Hilda was the proxy for Rex and the engagement took place at Stratford jewellers in Hastings – Rex had worked for Mr Stratford before the war.

In 1940 Ruth and family had the distress of waiting to hear what had happened to Rex, who for three months from April was posted as missing in France. In fact the Germans had overrun his unit south of Dunkirk at Doullens and he had been transported to a Polish labour camp; a postcard from the Red Cross brought the news in August. The photos of camp life which came from Poland to the family every so often, were organised by the SS for propaganda purposes to show good treatment. The reality was very different and some events such as the many days' rail trip to Poland with everyone wedged standing room only in carriages, Rex seldom spoke about, except in his sleep.

Ruth Pearson in the Womens Land Army 1942 and 1944

Ruth's mother refused to sign papers for Ruth to go into the Women's Auxiliary Air Force (WAAF), so she went into the Women's Land Army instead, aged just over 17 in 1941.

Ruth's work in the Land Army (shown above in her uniform) first took her to Herne Bay for six weeks' training in dairy farming including learning how to milk by hand; then on to a farm at Challock near Charing in Kent. There, she and another girl Mary Cork milked the dairy herd at 5 am in the morning, then breakfast at 8 am. After mucking out the cowsheds, it would be milking again at 3pm in the afternoon. For the rest of the day they picked leeks and potatoes in the fields during the winter;

and harvested hay in the summer – the hay had to be collected by hand because the combined harvester had not yet been introduced. The two of them were relatively fortunate to be billeted with a friendly and kind couple in a bungalow half a mile from the farm: more comfortable than the massive hostel at Herne Bay! Back in Gravesend, however, Ruth's mother Ellen Wood (*née* Bratton) was having a torrid time with bombing of the town, as she writes in the following letter:

How are you down that way with the air raids? I hope you are safe. we do not get much peace here, sometimes as many as six sirens a day. and from seven in the evening until about six in the morning we have to spend in the shelter, as the planes come in one after another and the barrage is terrible, at the moment I am writing this letter in the shelter I do not have time for anything as I do not get home from work until six o'clock, trusting this letter will find you safe & well.

Yours sincerely

E M Wood

Ruth had to accompany the animals to the market in Ashford for auction – she recalls ribald remarks in the auction ring about whether she or the bull was for sale. Over 70 years before the 'Me Too' campaign about harassment, Ruth told the farmer off and he did not repeat these unwelcome comments.

One of the highlights was the visit of Princess Marina to boost the morale of the Land Army in the Charing area: but Ruth appears in none of the photos!

Ruth and Battle

In late 1945 Ruth came to Battle to live with Rex's mother and father at 24 Wellington Gardens (built in 1920), although she was still technically enlisted in the Land Army. She would have been surrounded by the large concrete tank traps at Wellington Gardens, installed there as part of the town's anti-invasion defences.

She remembers well the Towers Hotel – used as a girls' school before the war, and then by Canadian troops. Ruth recalls the two butchers – Hollands and Lee; the grocers in Lower Lake; Allworks; the clockmakers where the bookshop now is; and the pie shop Poveys on the corner of Mount Street where the florists is today: Rex's mother knew the pie shop and family well. The saddlers in Mount Street was often used, as was Huntly's grocers and the off licence, quips Ruth. Tony Emeleus, the High Street chemist, stands out in Ruth's memory: 'and what can I do for you', he would say in a Finnish accent, dispensing amazing concoctions such as a special Emeleus joint liniment usable on horses and humans. She used the Senlac cinema complete with its blackout strips, and the Martins Oak surgery but Ruth recalls Dr Davidson as being 'rather scary'. At the same time, however he was known to be kind, for example when he treated injured German pilots. For recreation Ruth attended evening classes in pottery at Claverham where the school now is, in 1946.

After getting married Rex and Ruth lived in Battle until 1956, first in a prefab just beyond Lower Lake and then at 40 Wellington Gardens. Ruth remembers many parties and an active social life at the Drill Hall, including the one below in 1947, the photograph of which started off many historical projects some 70 years later in 2017 when found in the Museum archives.

What brought together Ruth (centre), Mary Thompsett (right) and Jean Blackman (left) for this photo was that their husbands had all been in the Royal Engineers and had met at the Milton Barracks in Gravesend. Mary's aunt also lived next to Ruth's aunt in her home town of Swanscombe. It was in Gravesend that Ruth had met Mary Thompsett. Ruth remembers there was a sizeable contingent of Canadian soldiers at the dance, and many there had had 'one over the eight'. Mary's father in law Harry Thompsett was one of the Home Guard anti-invasion Special Patrols, with a hideout in Telham. The threat of German invasion in the first half of the War was seen as an imminent danger, Ruth recalls.

Ruth remembers well the wartime food rationing caused by German sinking of ships destined for Britain. Every household, including Rex's parents at 24 Wellington Gardens, had a ration book of coupons for various types of food, which the shopkeeper crossed through. There were no supermarkets in Battle then, or anywhere else, so shoppers had to queue up at several shops to complete the weekly shop. Queuing subsequently became a British tradition. Rations were very small, for example four ounces of bacon per person per week, and one egg. The butter ration was 2 ounces a week, about a quarter of the pack to be found in a shop today. Bananas and oranges were almost unknown. Meat was in very short supply, even though Battle had three butchers at the time as Ruth recalls. She also recalls that after the war some vegetarian options were tried, for example Lord Woolton's Pie (after the Minister of Food) comprising potatoes, swede, cauliflower and spring onions. There were no allotments in Wellington Gardens because it was surrounded by tank traps to protect the civil defence entre nearby, but there were many areas of Battle dug up for vegetables. Clothes were in short supply and rationed so 'make do and mend' entered the English language. Even wedding cakes were affected: use of icing was banned so instead, many couples had a wedding cake with a cardboard cover – decorated with crepe paper and flowers – for the top of the fruit cake. Ruth and Rex had a lovely fruit cake made by Rex's mother's neighbour.

End of the war

For Rex the highlight of his return to England was seeing Hastings from the air – the Dakota pilot diverted specially. Rex and Ruth were reunited at 24 Wellington Gardens in May 1945. He was so emaciated and weak that when she flung her arms around him he fell over. He needed three months' convalescence in the now-disappeared Buchanan Hospital in St Leonards, to recover his strength. But informal notes , such as the one below, exchanged with the hospital staff showed his sense of humour was undiminished!

Like many couples, Ruth and Rex did not know how they would get on after 5 years' absence but, as Ruth remarks, drily, 'we were alright'. Yet, Ruth notes, Rex was much older from his experiences, beyond just the passage of five years. With his typical humour Rex, when asked where they met, would reply 'In a blackout'. So for Rex and Ruth, VE Day was a non-event: Ruth spent it in Challock because she still had Land Army work to do ; and Rex was in the Buchanan Hospital at Hastings, convalescing. Ruth recalls with some bitterness that after all Rex had been through, he was required to remain enlisted for a year after he returned.

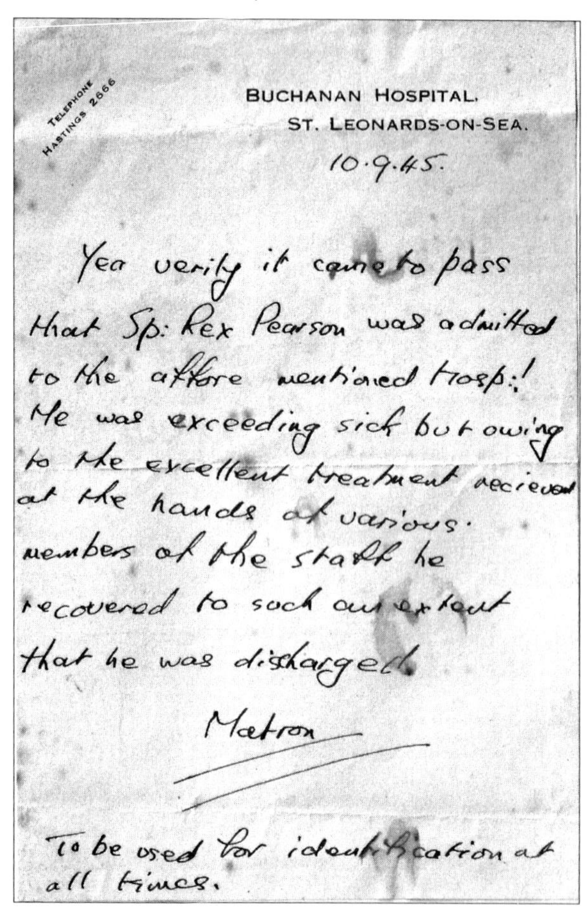

TELEPHONE HASTINGS 2666

BUCHANAN HOSPITAL.
ST. LEONARDS-ON-SEA.

10.9.45.

Yea verily it came to pass that Sp: Rex Pearson was admitted to the affore mentioned Hosp:! He was exceeding sick but owing to the excellent treatment recieved at the hands of various members of the staff he recovered to such an extent that he was discharged.

Matron

To be used for identification at all times.

But things looked up when they were married at St Mary's Church Battle, on 8th December 1945 (picture opposite). The Rt Rev Wilfred Youard came out of retirement as Dean of Battle to marry them because Rex had been in the Church Choir as man and boy. Ruth's wedding dress was hired for £5 from stock in America made available, under a special scheme, to Land Girls.

Rex and Ruth's lives after the war

It was common for returning servicemen to find it hard to settle back into the civilian world. In Rex's case he also liked to move on when he had mastered a job – he needed a challenge. Doubtless his dreadful wartime experience unsettled him as well. His love was cabinet-making and Ruth's house is full of the furniture he made. But the premature death of his father Reginald in 1946 put an end to that ambition: they had planned to create a furniture-making business, but Reginald died three years after he narrowly escaped death in the 1943 bombing of the newsagents in Battle High Street. He had been working in the workshop at the back of the newsagents when the bomb hit, with the resulting damage shown in the family snap below.

He was relatively uninjured when the workshop collapsed around him but he was never the same again after the shock.

So Ruth and Rex's lives took a different turn. After taking a job with Judds the furniture removers (where the Battle Abbey School extension is, opposite the Abbey), Rex then worked for Tills the general store for a while but that did not work out because the shop was not well managed at the time. Then Rex became a rent collector for Battle Town Council. In 1956 he and Ruth moved to Maidstone when he got a job in the local council there. He ended up as buyer for a building firm called Cox Brothers in Maidstone. On retirement Rex and Ruth eventually moved back to the Battle area, living in Catsfield for 20 years, then they moved back to Battle itself in 2001. It was in these years that Rex made three carvings: one of the insignia of the Royal Sussex Regiment (on display in Battle Museum); one of his own regiment the Royal Engineers; and one of the Womens' Land Army. It was not until 1960 that Rex felt able to put his wartime memories to paper and he did so again in 1992, with the help of local historian Stan Elliott. Rex died in 2004 aged 83.

DIFFICULT POSTINGS : THE WAR STORY OF SERGEANT WALLY PETERS

Wally Peters was a mechanic at Vicarys in Battle High Street when he was called up in 1940. In a six year stint with the Army, he served in many tricky areas of the conflict: the Middle East battle against Rommel and the Monte Cassino assault in southern Italy against the German garrison. Then there was a posting to Klagenfurt in Austria, where the British had to deal with retreating Germans and advancing Yugoslav partisans in such a way as to defuse a potentially explosive situation. Finally Wally was at Wolfsberg, dealing with the harrowing task of doomed Russian PoWs being forced to return home. Here is Wally's story, written by him in 1995 and brought to us by kind permission of his daughter Linda Anonchans.

Training and duties in the UK 1940-42

"I was called up for military service in March 1940 and remained in the Army until 1946. My Army career started with a limited period of military training at Woolwich Barracks in London. I was then sent to the Lea-Francis factory at Isleworth, on a mechanics' training course. After a few weeks of what should have been a three month course, I was then engaged on overhauling Norton motorcycle gearboxes. On completing the so-called training course, I was then attached to the 1st Battalion Royal West Kent Infantry, who were billeted at the Aston Villa football ground in Birmingham, following their return from Dunkirk. I was promoted to Lance Corporal. Having made up its losses from France, the Battalion moved to Corsham in Wiltshire, to guard an ammunition dump.

"The threat of a German invasion saw us moved to the Isle of Wight for several months, and then into the Aldershot area for a while before moving to Highclere near Newbury Berkshire. Whilst there I was promoted to Sergeant. My salary was increased from 1/0 to 3/6d a day. I was then transferred to 2nd Battalion Lancashire Fusiliers, stationed at Boscombe.

After months of training schemes, I then moved up to Langholm in Scotland, and later to the Bridge of Allan, Stirling. Whilst there, we carried out modifications to motor transport, notably waterproofing, along with extensions to exhaust and inlet pipes.

Manchester Port

"On completion I went down to the Birkenhead area, ferrying vehicles to the docks for loading onto ships. Personnel were reorganised: the 78th division had been formed from the 11th, 36th and 1st Guards Infantry Brigade. Then we went back to Greenock, shortly to board the ships that had been loaded at Birkenhead. The ship that I boarded was the 8000 ton 'Manchester Port'"– shown above.

"We were to spend three weeks at sea, during which we were told that our destination was to be Algeria. We landed in an area of Algiers – apart from some diplomatic incident with the French because they were not happy to see us – and the landing was fairly successful, such that we gained the use of Blida airfield.

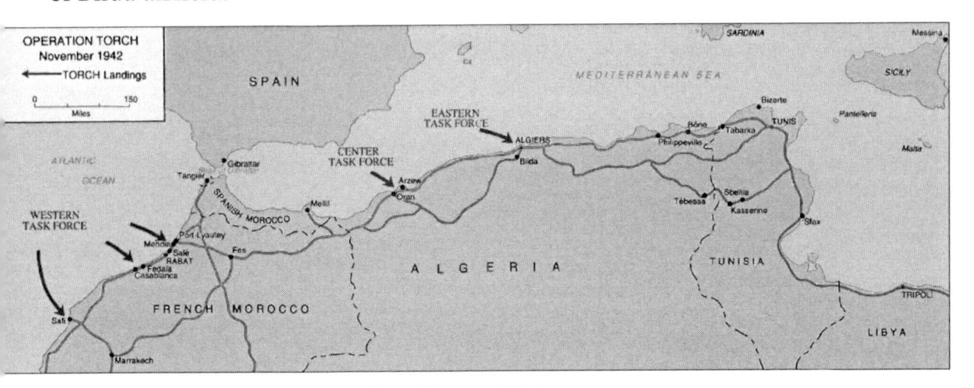

Landing at Algiers

[*Wally in his account underplays what a dangerous amphibious landing this was (shown above), part of Operation Torch (November 1942) led by US forces, with support from the British. Algeria was nominally held by Vichy France, who were co-operating with the Germans back home, so they did not welcome the US/British arrival. Another reason for a cool French reception was that in 1940 the British had shelled the Vichy French Navy at the Algerian port of Mers el Kebir, when it refused to guarantee that the Germans would not be able to use it. Over 1,000 French died in the ensuing bombardment.*]

"Progress through Algeria was fairly straightforward, apart from thunderstorms, heavy rain and a lack of home comforts. We passed through numerous villages and the towns of Setif and Constantine. We entered Tunisia at Souk el Arba, on to Seja and the heights of Testour and Teboursoak on the outskirts of Medjez-al-Bab, where we met the Germans and things started to get rough. After the capture of Medjez, the wet weather persisted. We then became bogged down for the winter, on a mountainous area called Oud Zarga, Sidi Niser, Toubousouk and Beja. Four or five months later, having been strengthened by reinforcements, we fought a successful campaign resulting in the capture of Tunis and the end of the African campaign.

[*The US and British forces took Tunis on 6 May 1943 after fierce German resistance and counter-attacks. Many historians of the period regard this as the pivotal victory of the war, enabling the Allies then to push on to invasion of Italy through Sicily.*]

Sgt Peters on far right in Egypt

"During this period I was carrying out vehicle maintenance in the field on the following: Austin and Bedford 15cwt and three ton trucks, Morris Commercial anti-tank gun portees, BSA motorcycles, Bren Gun carriers (Ford V8 engines) and Jeeps.

Invasion of Italy 1943

"Whilst in Tunis, the 1st Army was transferred to the 8th Army, which had come up through the desert. Preparation was then made for the invasion of Sicily[1], across the Mediterranean from Hammermet to Amola in SW Sicily, and on up the east coast via Mt Etna to Messina, ready for the attack on Italy itself.

The next move was across the Straits of Messina to Reggio on the toe of Italy, following the 5th British and 1st Canadian divisions, and to make our way up the Adriatic coast, across the River Sangro. Before we crossed the river we called for air support from the Americans, but unfortunately they did not seem to know the South from the North, and we were bombed. We were then pulled out to cross the country to the Naples area to support the American 5th Army, together with New Zealanders and Polish troops for the assault on the Cassino defences.

[The River Sangro crosses the Italian mainland from coast to coast and was used by the Germans as the basis for their Gustav Line, blocking access to the north of Italy and the route up to Germany. It was not until 1944 that it was finally secured. The report of 'friendly fire' at this juncture cannot be verified from other sources.]

The German troops had a commanding position from the monastery at Monte Cassino and the surrounding heights (below).

1 Codenamed Operation Husky. In his Division, Sergeant Peters landed in the south west of Sicily

Monte Cassino

Consequently we were unable to move about until daylight or we could have been mortared. I was at Cassino for about four weeks[2] until we captured the Monastery and the Germans retreated. The town of Cassino was flattened.

[*Allied bombing demolished the Abbey at Monte Cassino, now restored. This was one of the fiercest battles of the war, involving removal of German troops from a hilltop fortress.*]

Problems in Austria 1945-46

"After Cassino we moved on to Rome, Orvito and Cortina and at this stage our losses in men and material warranted the Division's withdrawal back down to the south of Italy and we then boarded the *Empress of India* at Taranto for a voyage to Port Said in Egypt. In Egypt we camped at Ismalia

2 Early 1944

and after a few months re-equipping and leave in Cairo, we went back to Italy. We then went into action in the Florence area and travelled through the mountains into the Lombardy Plain, through Padova and Udine to reach the Austrian border at Villach where there were thousands of PoWs, displaced persons and refugees who had to be contended with. A short stay in Klagenfurt then on to Vienna, taking over barracks that had been occupied by a Mongolian unit whose lavatorial habits could be compared with animals, hygiene being non-existent. Another short stay there and on to Wolfsberg[3] on the Yugoslav frontier where the unit's unpleasant task was to force some Russian troops , who had been fighting with the German Army, on to trains bound for Russia, where they knew they would be in for a rough time. A number of them committed suicide, rather than go back.

[*The Russians of whom Wally speaks may have been the ROA or Russian Liberation Army, who fought with the Germans against the Red Army and were led by General Vlasov. Or more likely they may have been the Russian Cossacks, trapped in the Austria/Yugoslavian area by the advancing Red Army against whom they had fought. There were many other groups subject to forced repatriation to the Soviet Union, probably numbering millions. These groups were repatriated by the British to the then Soviet Union arising from an agreement between Stalin, Churchill and Roosevelt, confirmed at the Yalta Conference in 1945. The Soviets released British and American prisoners in exchange. On return to the Soviet Union, the leaders were executed and the rest of the men given long sentences in gulags.*]

Return to England

"In March 1946 I returned to England, travelling by train, and discharged from the Army with a good reference.

On his return to Battle, Wally continued working at Vicarys from April 1946 until his retirement in March 1982. He married Molly in 1948, having Linda Anonchans *née* Peters, as their daughter."

3 In Austria

THE STORY OF ONE LOCAL HERO

The extraordinary exploits of Squadron Leader John Shore MC AFC

Even among the many brave exploits of Allied airmen in the Second World War, the story of Squadron Leader John Shore MC AFC, a Battle man, is extraordinary. In his own words, in the account which follows, John Shore describes – in a version not hitherto published – his rare 'home run' in 1941 from Stalag Luft I at Barth in northern Germany. This introduction explains something about John's eventful and tragically short life.

John Shore

Born on 29th April 1917, John moved to Battle in 1921 when his father Walter became proprietor of the Watts Bridge Garage, a petrol station which used to be at the junction of Canadia Road and London Road. After local schooling, John went to St Lawrence College in Ramsgate where he excelled at sports, shooting and the Officer Training Corps.

Back at Battle, John is remembered as a hyperactive person. He was an enthusiastic scouter, being the cub master at the Battle Pack. He was to continue his love of scouting in the RAF when he became a founder member of the Air Scouts, receiving an award from the Scouting Association. On leaving college in 1935, John worked in the servicing department of

Vicarys Garage (run by H G Seymour) in Battle: he loved fast cars and driving them very fast. But, doubtless enthused by the flying aces of the 1930s, his main aim was to join the RAF.

John joined the RAF in 1936 and as war came he found himself as an above – average pilot in Bomber Command: a high risk occupation in which 60% were killed, wounded or became PoWs. On 17 November 1939, at St Mary's Church, John married a Battle girl, Rosa Phyllis Salmon, who was a nurse at the Royal East Sussex Hospital in Hastings and went by the nickname 'Jo'.

In January 1941, John joined No 9 Squadron flying Wellingtons on bombing raids over Germany. It was on 27th March 1941 that John set off from home for that day's raid, promising Jo that he would return come what may. One of John's crew that night was Les 'Cookie' Long, who, three years later, was a leading member of the Great Escape but sadly was shot by the Gestapo. John and his crew had engine trouble on the way back from bombing Cologne and were captured by the Germans after a forced landing in Holland. Now, John tells us in his own words (which have come to us from H G Seymour's son Peter) typed by his mother, how he escaped from Stalag Luft I and got back to Jo in England via Sweden: a rare 'home run' for which he was awarded the Military Cross (MC).

John Shore's story of his 'home run' from Germany to England in 1941

Forced landing

"In the late afternoon of 27th March 1941 I said 'Cheerio' to my wife and she said 'Come back safely', for of course she knew I would be out that night. I had told her that I should always try to get back to her even from a prison camp.

That night we were briefed for rather a largish raid on Cologne and were over the target area for two and a half hours and were on our way back when at 12,000 feet my starboard engine packed up and five seconds later the other stopped. It was a dark night, cloud about 4/10 and very quiet – all the more so because of the suddenly silenced engines.

I was captain of the aircraft' K' for Katie and had five crew – Flying Officer Long as 2nd pilot; Sgt Tomkins (Tommy), Observer; Sgt Beeves, W/T Operator; Sgt Griffiths (Griff), Rear Gunner; Sgt Parkins, Front Gunner and 2nd Wireless Operator.

Vickers Wellington

I think the petrol tanks were holed, for no matter what I did I couldn't get the engines to go again, so out we had to go. Griff went first at 8,000 feet with a cheery 'Goodbye sir, happy landings', then the others in succession. Poor old Katie was going down like a brick and I wondered if the others had a horrid sinking feeling in their tummies like I had as I jumped.

I didn't get out till 1,500 feet, almost too late. Out into the dark, turning over and over I tried to find my ripcord which I had lost as I jumped from the aircraft. It was the loose type and so was not attached to the harness, but I found it and pulled, and sent up a thankful prayer when I saw the canopy billowing above me. Only just in time for it seemed that I almost immediately came to earth with a bang and another 'thank God' that it was earth and not water.

Getting to safety

I lay still a few minutes to recover for I felt bruised all over and hoped I had broken no bones but found I had only sprained an ankle. I daren't remove my boot as it acted as a support and I feared I might not get it on again. I had landed just beside some water but could not see what it was, and started to hobble away from it.

The going was extremely hard (I hadn't realised I was so tired) and then I found I was climbing a bank which I gathered was a canal or river embankment, and at the top was barbed wire. I then saw that I was still attached to my parachute which I had completely forgotten, so no wonder it was heavy going! I detached it, kept a length of rope for further use, then rolled down the bank again, gathered up the parachute and tried to push it into the water. I do not know how successful this was, but I hoped it was hidden for the time being.

I then crawled up the bank again and saw a flashing light which I knew from former sorties was in Holland, and could see a fire, two or three miles away, which I guessed must be old Katie. Well, she had done her best!

"Katie" – crashed

It was about 12.30 hours now and as I could see nothing, I decided to walk until I could find a dwelling and try my luck. I made slow progress and kept on for about three hours. I could hear the chiming of a clock in the distance which I took to indicate that I was nearing a village church. We had been told to try and find a padre if possible, but I knew I couldn't do any more. Suddenly I saw a cottage and went up close and picked up a handful of gravel and threw it at an upper window, with no result. Looking around I saw a cattle shed and went to it, my object being to get a drink. I could hear an animal inside but, of course, it might have been a bull, so I decided not to risk that, although some milk would have been welcome, so I felt along the wall and found a stand pipe, and gratefully had a drink. Then I saw a straw stack and lay down under that, and immediately fell asleep.

In the morning I heard the farmer come out and I hobbled over to him as best I could. Then came difficulty: he could only speak Dutch and I English, but he understood that I was English.

He took me indoors and his wife gave us breakfast, while he went out – I thought to get the police, for there was a good reward for captured enemies. However in about half an hour he returned with the local padre who could speak moderate English. I asked him if I could hide up until my ankle had healed and I could then move on. He told me that it was unlikely that the farmer could risk it. I remarked that I didn't see much risk but he answered that I had no idea of conditions existing in Holland right now. The Dutch themselves were often astonished, the padre said: 'this farmer has given you breakfast and according to the Nazis that was wasting Reich food, the punishment for which is imprisonment. He has also fetched me, instead of the police or Germans and thus forfeited 1000 guilders, his reward for a prisoner, and should it be found out that he has sheltered you, it would mean a concentration camp. If you were found in his haystack, he would be shot there in his yard.'

In the face of this I asked what he proposed to do with me, and he said he would take me to a friend of his and we set off. With his support I got along better but since it appeared unlikely that my presence could be kept a secret – the milkman had passed us and greeted the padre – I was glad to accept a lift in a market cart. I found that they knew the latest news from England, hearing it apparently by illegal means. I had passed the house to which he took me, the night before, but as it stood well back from the road, behind trees, I had not noticed it in the dark. It would have simplified matters enormously had I gone there first, as the owner could and would have hidden me. However I might not have managed to get away from there, and 'all things work together for good'.

Major Van Gombert told me that he and his wife had been watching a burning aircraft in the distance the night before, not knowing what it was and thought they heard me pass, and did so wish to come and see, but of course the curfew was on and it might have been a German. They were kindness itself and offered me a wash and shave for which I was grateful and meanwhile the Major sent for his own doctor. In the bathroom was a suit of clothes and all a man needed in his pocket: knife, watch, compass and pocket book with money, obviously for my benefit, but it would have been madness to avail myself of the opportunity with my injured foot, and it would probably have spoiled another man's chance, so I could only thank them.

They got out a map and showed me where we were, told me where I could find a hidden ladder, and which window to knock at should I ever get away from prison camp and come their way. He then rang the police to report. I will add here that as long as I remained in Germany they continued to keep me supplied with parcels. I gave the Major my ring and watch, thinking I would prefer him and his wife to keep them for me rather than risk a Nazi pinching them. After the war, when my uncle happened to be General Commanding of the Allied Forces in Holland,he was of course glad to get in touch with this kind family and I received back my ring and watch.

Taken into custody and interrogation

By this time the German police arrived and I was taken to a police station, where to my deep gratitude I found four of my crew. Tommy had disappeared but we were not in the least concerned. He had all the food and could speak good French – we felt certain he could hide up and get through. As a matter of fact he was still missing when I returned home but I was able to comfort his family and later my confidence was justified as he was reported safe in Switzerland where he was interned throughout the rest of the war.

We were closely questioned but only gave the minimum of information, that is: our names, rank, numbers, and home addresses for the Red Cross. We were then put in a lorry and taken to Amsterdam; quite an interesting journey as we saw a tremendous amount of damage done during the fighting before the occupation period. Poor Holland! In Amsterdam we were taken to the barracks, put into separate cells and again interrogated, and all our personal things were taken away. We were asked to empty our pockets but we were not searched. It was about 17.00 hours and I was rather empty and was relieved when some supper arrived, consisting of bread, some fairly substantial sausage, and a hot drink which they called 'coffee'.

Next day we were taken with the crew of another bomber to Frankfurt-am-Main where we were put into the reception block at Dulag Luft. We were stripped to our underclothes and issued with bedclothes and some bread and cheese and 'coffee' for supper. My clothes were returned to me the next day and although even the linings had been ripped, they still had not found my precious maps.

Dulag Luft PoW camp

I heard the interrogator in the next room for two hours and feared that the Sergeant was quite unconsciously giving away a lot of information. The officer then came into see me and was deliberately friendly, offering me a cigarette which I refused as I did not smoke. I only answered the questions that were necessary and not any others. He seemed a bit peeved that I was obstinate on this point, as the information, he said, was 'only for the Red Cross'. I couldn't have any idea as to why the Red Cross should want to know my squadron and the name of the Squadron Commander. They would know that already.

We all exercised in the same ground although officers and other ranks had separate sleeping quarters; therefore I was able to ask vital questions of my crew. They had apparently given nothing away and there was no subsequent interrogation.

I was issued with a Polish greatcoat, tunic and trousers. They were rather astonished that I insisted on a greatcoat that was much too long for me. It would easily have fitted a 6' 4" man but I said it would be warmer. I managed to stick to this wonderful garment throughout my incarceration, and by the simple expedient of a six inch hem, made good extra pockets for possible escape material.

My swollen ankle meanwhile was getting better. I kept on it as much as I could and gave my parole at this camp so that I could go for walks. The food and accommodation were much better than those we found at our next stop, Stalag Luft I. At Dulag I heard of an attempt by 18 prisoners to build a tunnel, but unfortunately it was not a success. Among those men were Wing Commanders Day and Hyde; and Major Dodge whom I admired immensely. Discipline was rather lax and there was no searching of rooms. We were allowed to write three letters and four postcards a month, and morale was high. When I moved from Dulag there were 105 PoWs in the camp. I had managed to collect some tins of food. Parcels were issued communally and I was paid 32 marks a month. When we wished to discuss escaping matters, we did so in the compound.

First escape attempt

We were given 48 hours' notice before leaving and I took all my kit except for the Polish tunic and trousers. My flying boots had been returned with my own uniform. As my parole was out of date I was determined to try for a getaway, for we had no idea where we were being taken. On April 15th at 08.00 hours, a bus was brought. We were marched out to it and checked but not searched, then taken to Frankfurt goods yard where a special coach was standing. After the train started I apparently had a bad attack of diarrhoea which continued until I had managed to loosen all the screws in the lavatory window.

I had chosen a seat in the carriage next to the window so that I could watch the country. There were maps in the carriage and we saw we went towards Berlin, but my idea was to get out and make towards the Swiss frontier so I wanted to do it soon, even though it was daytime. As we were running through wooded countryside I decided to try my luck and so went back to my unscrewed window and when the train was on an outside curve, I pushed out my greatcoat and followed immediately. I certainly did not expect to drop so hard or so noisily. I was heard and the train stopped, but my ankle failed me. I tried to clamber up the bank but a corporal shot at me and others yelled 'put your hands up or they'll kill you', and so ended a fiasco of an attempt at escape.

The corporal was very annoyed and picked up my greatcoat, but showed no apparent surprise at its weight and actually returned it to me after he had helped me back into the train. Well, that put paid to any further attempt on the journey and for some weeks to come, for I knew that I must get my foot into good trim before I tried again.

Arrival at Stalag Luft I Barth

It took half an hour for the train to restart and so we missed our connection at Kassal, the next one starting at 6 pm. We were put in a corridor carriage and locked in, but were let out at Berlin for a wash. Early next morning we went through the city and saw much damage on the way, our journey ending on 17th April at Barth, which was somewhere near to Rostock on the Baltic Sea.

Stalag Luft I

We were marched to Stalag Luft I and put in the Sergeants' Mess and then five at a time were taken to the Officers' compound and our pockets searched, but not very thoroughly. We were given a number and issued with bedding and a bowl, with knife, spoon and fork. The rations were very poor and at first Red Cross parcels arrived, about one per man a month but this improved later. We were not allowed to keep the tins, which were opened, although the food inside was not examined.

Wing Commander Day was senior officer and he often had to complain about the stupid punishment meted out for minor delinquencies. For instance, the lights might be shut off at 5 o'clock and we were told that the power had failed. Of course we teased the guards in every possible way, and acted sometimes like small boys. It is extraordinary to think that mature men confined in a camp as we were, could bother to think up such crazy ideas. One that appealed especially to us was, when on parade, to flick the helmet of the guard in front of me with my finger nail. It must have sounded like a thunder clap! Somehow they never picked on me as the culprit and of course everyone else denied it hotly.

There was an anti-Nazi officer in the camp and he kindly warned us whenever there was going to be a search, which was once every ten or fourteen days. We used to take a book, or something to eat, and were marched to the Sergeants' Mess. At first the search parties left our room in an awful mess, but on the Wing Commander's complaining to the American who visited the camp, they tidied up after this.

In August I made another abortive attempt to get away while the Americans were about. I had obtained a civvy suit from a kindly guard to whom I gave my ration of cigarettes and some things from my home parcels which were coming regularly then. Another man got away but I was recognised at the main gateway and incarcerated in solitary confinement for eight days.

My guard had a beautiful Alsatian dog always with him. I wanted to see if he would obey me, so I made good friends with the guard who allowed me to pat the dog which also treated me as a friend, and very soon obeyed my commands. However, the poor man was annoyed because I insisted on my full quota of exercise for I wanted to strengthen my foot, and he had to accompany me.

I heard that our *Hauptmann* (German Commander) was having special searches – probably because I had hidden my civvies so carefully, and when I returned to circulation I found we were turned out of our rooms to the Sergeants' Mess at 08.30 hrs in the morning till 18.30 hrs at night and so 170 of us got no exercise. We were allowed out to the lavatory at stated times. This went on for ten days in succession with only a Sunday break. Then we had four days' peace followed by another ten days' searches. The

German guards got very annoyed about this for they were fourteen hours on duty, and then their Hauptmann was moved away – much to our relief.

I put two or three escape plans before the committee but they were turned down and I suppose I earned the nickname of "death" by which I came to be known.

The escape attempt takes shape

Now I knew I must soon make a determined effort because I did not wish to travel on foot in the winter and F/Officer James[1] proposed to dig a tunnel from the incinerator. Actually, they did not burn the stuff here but it was emptied on the first Monday in the month. It was built of brick and divided in two, about 6 ft from the wire fence, the other side of which was the football field of the Ack Ack station near to us.

John Shore at Stalag Luft I with Jimmy James

1 "Jimmy" James who later took part in the Great Escape from Stalag Luft III and survived.

The plan was to make an entrance in the roof over the 'wet' rubbish side and dig from there. The roof was used as a grandstand for the PoWs to watch the football which was played every day at 10.30 hrs so the cover of the hold could be easily kicked aside and the tunnellers drop in, while the other men kept us hidden. We carefully removed some bricks from between the two parts to dispose of the dirt into the cinder side and then made a start to tunnelling through the floor. James and I worked every day except Sunday from 10.30 to 17.00 hrs.

It was arranged that 12 men should climb to the top of the rubbish bin to hide our exit. The rubbish was noticed to be getting more than usually full and orders were to clear it. One man noticed that it was mostly dirt but the corporal apparently did not heed and we saw all evidence of our work being carted away, and had no doubt that we should be discovered. Anyway we decided to knock off work for a few days. They had been told to look out for people hiding in the rubbish cart and other searches were carried out. After a day or so's digging the stench was a bit overpowering, although we left the hatch a little open. Somebody suggested a little chloride of lime and knew how to lay his hands on some. Fools that we were, forgetting that the gas dropped! Anyway we both got ill and I started to cough badly and spat blood. I daren't report sick or I might have been removed.

When we returned to work we carefully pushed up sticks to the surface hoping to give ourselves more air. I found I was suffering severely from claustrophobia. We were working in a tunnel which was to be only 25 feet long, but it was only big enough to crawl along and we did not try to shore it up at all. We dug with our spoons and knives and put the earth on two small boards which the man working behind pulled back and at the same time sending the empty board forward. For this my parachute rope came in handy.

It was a good thing that I had two pairs of trousers so could change after work and wash them, for we got very dirty. I was more than thankful when the work underground was finished and we knew we had only to push up a thin layer of earth left on top of the boards, which we used to hold it up.

John Shore at Stalag Luft I, front left

Here I must explain that my wife had sent me another uniform, so in odd times when it was safe, I did my best to turn my old uniform into a sort of civvy-suit by taking off pockets and letting in pleats at the back, and as our buttons were sewn on with plain ones on the wrong side, I sewed these on instead of the brass ones. For the cap, I used some of the thick black material in which the Red Cross sewed our parcels and made a peak with the black American cloth from the outside of an exercise book. The haversack I made from the bottom of a soft suitcase.

Now came the crucial time. Once the tunnel was completed we had to wait for an air raid during the moonless, or nearly so, nights after 15th October, when our flood lights would go out. Several of the other fellows wanted to use the tunnel after us, but I asked them to give us four hours' start if we were not found out. The guard was trebled during raids and it took about half an hour to get the extra guards in position. I allowed five minutes to get out of our huts and through the tunnel into the football field.

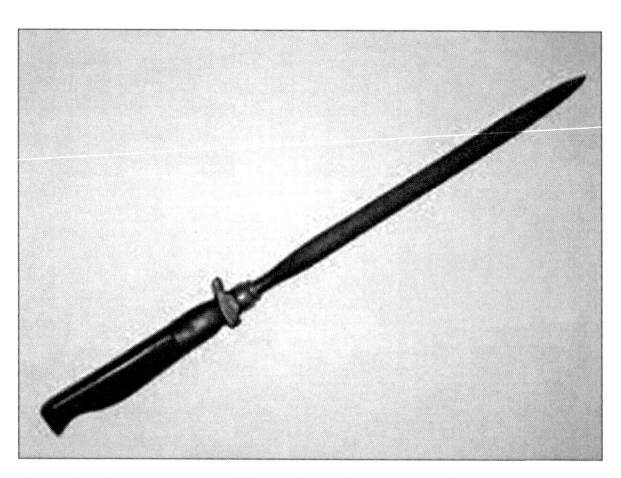

Dining knife converted by John Shore for digging the tunnel

We had to make trapdoors to get out of our huts. This needed some ingenuity. I made one from the dining room and James from his own room. On the 15th October, everything was ready, and we started to do nightly watches. I took from 22.00-24.00 hrs while another chap who was helping us named Newman took the watch from 24.00-02.00 hrs. I had my greatcoat and haversack. I was able to stand on some chairs and look out of the ventilator, as there was a large hole in the ceiling. This hole was made by one of the Ferrets (Germans who went round the camp searching). He had been crawling about over the room and the ceiling gave way. As this had not been mended, I was able to get at the ventilator and open it.

Escape

At 22.30 hrs on 19th October I heard aircraft and the lights went out. I went and warned Newman. I then started crawling through my trap door in the hut. Unfortunately I had put on my greatcoat, and when I was half-way through a German guard came along and nearly stepped on my coat. (I could not get back into the hut as my greatcoat had caught.) Luckily, the man did not notice me. He walked on for about 20 feet and then stood still watching something in one of the rooms. Then the guard at the gates started flourishing his torch to attract the attention of my guard, who walked over to the gate. I got up and walked after him making my footsteps coincide with his. I went along to James's hut and called him, and he came out just behind me. I then went across to the incinerator. I thought James would follow me, but as I walked across he may have mistaken me for a guard. I got into the incinerator and banged the door at regular intervals to attract his attention, but he did not come. I then went through the tunnel and found 6 inches of water in it. I had to remove my greatcoat and push it ahead of me, but couldn't keep either myself or it dry. I pushed up the trap door and put my head out. I could see the German guard talking to someone through the door of my hut and put my head out. I got out of the tunnel and went across the football field to the ditch which had been dug by the Germans, when it was decided to put another line of barbed wire in. (This had been done at the request of the Americans on the grounds that if the football field was enclosed with a double line of wire, it would be possible for the inmates of the camp to go there whenever they wanted, instead of having to go with a guard at certain specific times.)

I managed to crawl under the bottom wire, which was just below the ground surface and to push my haversack underneath as well. I made my way across the field. I then remembered that I had told James that I would wait half an hour for him in the wood to the West of the Flak School. While I was waiting and watching the camp I saw two lights, got 'wind-up' and went on. I set off down the main Barth-Planitz road, after squeezing lemon over my boots and clothing to destroy the scent – the Germans employed dogs.

The journey starts

I started walking towards Barth, passing one or two members of the Flak School on the way. I was getting near Barth when I heard a car coming up behind and I rushed about 30 yards off the road and lay down.

At the entrance to Barth there is an archway through which the road went. I saw what I took to be a lighted cigarette in the archway so I turned off to the right about twenty yards before I reached the archway. Luckily for me this small road rejoined the main road in the middle of Barth, which went to Martenshagen and there you get on to the main Velgast-Stralsund railway line. The road goes due east. I marched on down this road. It was then about 03.00 hrs. I arrived just outside Stralsund at about 06.30hrs and decided that it would be best to lie up for the day, so I retraced my steps to the wood I had noticed about a quarter of a mile back. About 10.00 hrs I was awakened by the songs of the Flak contingent marching into the wood for battery practice. There was irregular heavy fire about every three or four minutes.

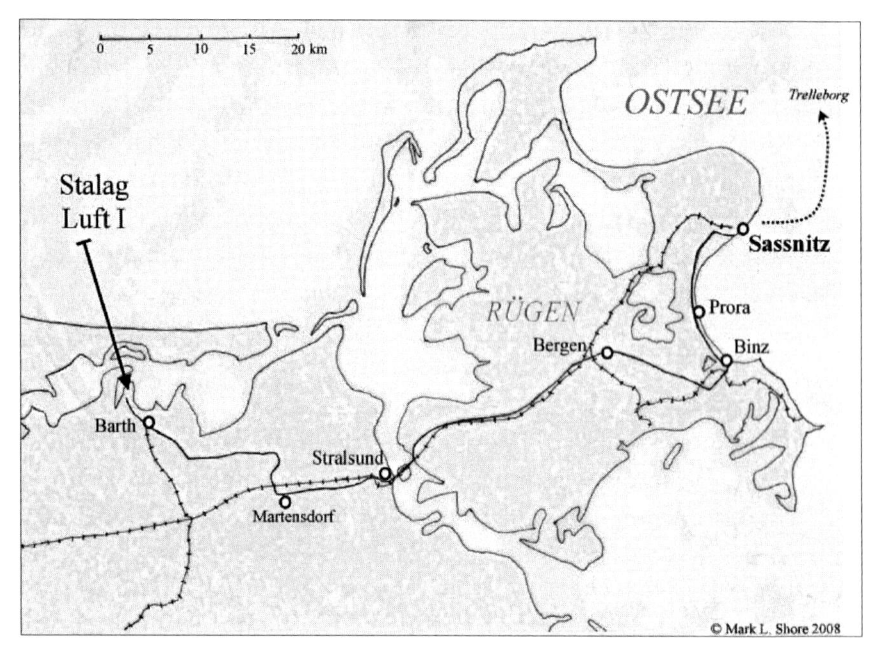

Escape route

I heard them march off for lunch and then again at about 17.00 hrs. I had unfortunately worn my own boots, which had been sent from home with some socks. A pair had been issued to me, but they were a bit small but I had broken them in and wore them without socks. Now I wished I still had them for my feet felt awful. I took off the boots and discarded them and put on gym shoes which I had brought with me.

I started off again at about 18.00 hrs and walked straight to Stralsund looking out for a bicycle all the time, but I could not manage to get hold of one. (All bicycles in Germany creaked for lack of any kind of lubricating oil.) I got down to the bridge at Stralsund and found that it was 35 miles to Sassnitz instead of 6 as I had thought. The bridge from the mainland on to Ruegen Island was guarded at both ends. There was nothing for it but to put a good face on it, and I walked steadily over, "Heil Hit-ling" at both ends! Apparently I didn't look too awful or they had not heard of a missing prisoner of war.

At this point I made an attempt to steal a bicycle, but a man came out of the hut, opposite to where the bicycle was standing, and called out to me! I ran away and hid behind a tree, the man went back into the hut and came out with a companion who had a lantern, but luckily they did not see me. I continued walking along the road and at about 06.30 hrs found a small wood where I hid up for the day and went to sleep. I managed to find some water in the wood when I left that night. I knew I was about five miles from Bergen. I decided to turn right through Bergen, instead of following the railway line through the centre of the town. After I had got through the town, I decided that I was on the wrong road so I came back into Bergen. I realised that my best course would have been to have followed the railway line and walked through the station at night, when, presumably, it would have been empty. I found that I was going East. I continued on this line as I thought I would hit the coast and could then follow it round, I did this and arrived at Binz which seemed to be a summer resort, then deserted. I heard the breakers and realised that I had arrived at the coast.

I walked on through Binz, then took a right turn, and then saw a signpost marked Sassnitz. After a time this road developed into an Autobahn. By this time my feet were getting very painful. I suddenly noticed a green and red light (railway lights). The main Autobahn road stopped and I continued on a grass track past some fisherman's houses. I noticed some fishing boats which I thought I might be able to use if I could not get on a ferry. It was beginning to get light, and I felt I ought to find somewhere to lie up for the day. First of all I dug myself into a haystack, but realised that this was not safe, so I went out on to the main road again. It was now about 07.30 hrs. A German sailor passed me and stared hard at me. Eventually I got to a plantation of fir and hid there, until about 19.00 hrs and then continued on down the road into Sassnitz.

Difficult choices at Sassnitz

The railway came into the main station and then down out of the station into the goods ferry yard. I turned off right on to a path which led down to the ferry, and walked along to the south end of the pier where I saw two big gantries. The ferry entrance was marked by two big arches. I got into a tarpaulin covered wagon marked with a Dutch name. I slept there for the night. The next day I wandered around in the truck. At about 13.30 hrs they started shunting the wagon, and I looked out to see that I was being taken back towards Sassnitz station. I jumped out hurriedly and had to leave all my food behind, with the exception of:

¼ lb of chocolate
2 tins of Horlicks tablets
2 tins of Ovaltine tablets
2 tins of Vitamin C
6 packets of chewing gum

I went back to the harbour again, it was then about 15.30 hrs. By this time I looked just like a German workman, very dirty and wearing a cap which I had made myself in the camp. I waited for a little time just above the harbour, trying to pick out the right wagon.

The boat came in and a line of passenger coaches came off. There was a line of coaches waiting in the siding. It was quite possible to walk around the harbour. There were one or two GAF[2] guards, the remaining men on duty were soldiers. I managed to get up underneath a Pullman train

2 GAF: German Air Force

hoping to be able to hang about there until the train was shunted onto the ferry. Unfortunately, the train started to move off towards the station, as had happened at my first attempt and I had to jump off. Incidentally, it is not advisable to try this as the Pullman coaches swing round corners and one is likely to be crushed. I ran up on to the bank just behind the track. This bank was covered with blackberry bushes and I was able to hide there. I watched the ferry boat leave at 16.30 hrs.

Sassnitz harbour and train terminal pre-war

I saw a Swedish three master standing at the main quay and I decided to try and get on her, but did not think that it would be safe to do so until about 19.00 hrs. Meanwhile, I had found some elderberries to quench my thirst. I found that I suffered quite a lot from lack of water, but I discovered later that there was a water hydrant in Sassnitz station.

I noticed that there were some houses at the top of the bank, and I clambered up hoping to find some water. I could not find any, and started walking down a narrow track which led to a rubbish heap. I had passed a woman on the way down and she looked at me very suspiciously as the track led to a cul-de-sac. When I arrived at the rubbish heap, I shrugged my shoulders, turned around and retraced my steps. When I passed the woman again she said something to me about the way to the station. I did not reply. I went back to my hiding place on the bank and was very sick.

A brush with the SS

At about 19.00 hrs I walked on to the Swedish boat. I saw a German SS looking at me and I asked the deckhand where the "captain" was. As the deckhand said the captain was not there I walked off the boat. There was another Swedish boat further on and some Danish fishing boats. I was walking along when another SS man came up and asked me what I wanted. I said "*Hans Kulture*" and "*Ich bin Schweder*" hoping that he would think that "*Hans Kulture*" was the name of my ship. I walked off towards the other Swedish boat followed by the SS man. Naturally, it was not the "*Hans Kulture*", so I said "*Nicht hier*" , shrugged my shoulders and slouched off again, still followed by the SS man. When we got opposite the Danish boats he asked me for my papers and I said "*Nicht veratehen*". The SS man then went and brought two Danes from the ship so that they could show me what he meant by papers. Luckily, a drunken Dane appeared and put his arms round me and the SS man.

Then the SS man turned to the other two Danes and asked them to produce their papers for me to see what he wanted, as he turned to speak to them I walked off. I then decided to wait for the Danish skippers to come back. As they passed me I said "Danish" to them, but they replied "*Nein, gute Deutsche*" I then went back past the railway line, and found the water hydrant, to which I have referred, just outside the station and had a drink. As I walked down towards the harbour I saw two Pullman coaches and got in one of them and had another drink and a wash in the lavatory. I was feeling rather despondent by then and got into a second class carriage and went to sleep, not caring much if I was discovered. I woke up at midnight and then again about 03.00 hrs and got out of the carriage as I suddenly realised that there might be a ferry about 04.30 hrs as well as at 16.30 hrs.

Ferry to Sweden

I scrambled into a tarpaulin covered truck filled with piping and looked out and saw the funnels of the ferry. A line of trucks was being taken on to the ferry and I jumped out of my truck, ran across the intervening 50 yards and managed to scramble on to a low truck which was passing at right angles. This truck contained a German lorry. The ferry then started off, it being then about 03.30 hrs.

During the voyage the trucks were not searched. I spent the time sitting in the driving cab of the lorry. When we arrived at Trelleborg a man on a bicycle noticed me sitting in the cab of the lorry. I managed to slip out and tried to get out of the goods yard, but, unfortunately, walked off in the wrong direction. I went through a gateway and was seen by a Swedish guard who came after me.

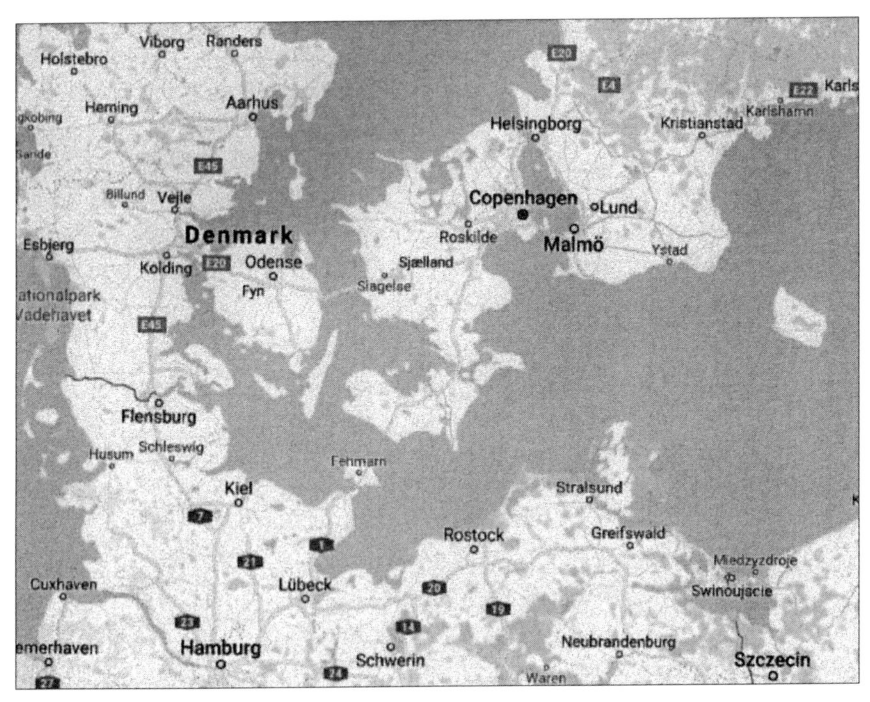

Geographical context of John Shore's escape. © *Googlemaps*

I was taken into a small office. I said I was an escaped PoW and must speak to the British Consul. I was told this was impossible. I then said that I must see the police. Two policemen came for me in a car and took me to the police station. No particulars were taken. A little later on, another man came in who spoke English. I was told that I had to give an account as to how I had got away and that this account would be forwarded to the Swedish Foreign Office. I wrote out an exceedingly brief account, but was told this would not do. I said I could not say any more until I saw the British Consul. They replied that I must write a full report before they could send for the Consul. I then wrote out a short report. They brought me food, very small meals at frequent intervals. They told me that I would be leaving for Stockholm at 12.00 hrs. They bought me a first class ticket and gave me 10kr. They took me down to the train and I was afraid that they might send me back to Sassnitz instead of putting me on the train to Stockholm, but luckily this did not happen.

Stockholm and freedom

I reached Stockholm at 6 o'clock next morning. It was Sunday, but I got a taxi, the driver of which looked at me very curiously. Granted I must have looked a sight after several nights sleeping out, with plenty of beard, and lack of food. However, he took me to the British Legation and I paid for the taxi with money supplied at Trelleborg. I had quite enjoyed the journey up in a first class sleeper with a German in the bunk above me. Unfortunately, he wanted the light out and this I just couldn't bear and was very glad to be able to insist on my own way at long last.

At the Legation when they once decided I was truly an escaped PoW everything possible was done for me and someone lent me a suit. I stayed a couple of nights at a hotel but found I was followed by a German. I had been told not to leave my room without an escort and was thankful to rest my feet which were very bad. They took a long time to heal and needed medical attention then and later. My skin also was covered with white rough patches due to lack of vitamins. I had managed to keep my teeth in pretty good condition by burning my bread and chewing the charcoal, but found I was excessively nervy for some months.

I returned to the United Kingdom by air to Edinburgh and wired my wife for money, asking her to meet me in London. It was wonderful to have been enabled to keep my promise to her and to be once more a free man. For some time, I was employed by the Air Ministry to visit Air Stations and lecture to those who might get into the same unfortunate position, and trust I may have been able to help with ideas. For this job I was supplied with a small aircraft. Later I was transferred to a research station in the West and spent some happy months there living in a caravan with my wife and little son."

Postscript

John got back to England in time for his second wedding anniversary: on that day, his old boss at Vicarys Garage, H G Seymour, drove Jo up to London to greet him. Now something of a celebrity, John had much to do. He toured RAF bases briefing aircrew about what to do if taken prisoner and how to escape. He was awarded the Military Cross on 13th March 1942 for his determination to escape and his courage and skill in doing so. The next month he joined the Research Department Flight of the Royal Aircraft Establishment and resumed flying, doing test pilot work for them, from RAF Churchstanton in Somerset. The work was highly dangerous, testing the War Office's experimental new anti-aircraft defences. In 271 flying hours he made 330 impacts with barrage balloon cables and there were several crash landings. John's nickname "Death", earned when he was a determined escaper, still applied. For his courage and considerable ability as a pilot, John was awarded the Air Force Cross (AFC) on 1st January 1944.

Even with all this going on, John still found time for family life. Jo joined him in Somerset and housed in a caravan near the RAF base, they enjoyed bringing up their first son, Rex, born in October 1942 – their second son Mark followed on 8th May 1945. John also attended the 1942 christening of Peter Seymour, son of the owner of Vicarys, H G Seymour, as shown below.

The last couple of years of the war saw John Shore in a variety of roles. He advised on a training film *Information Please,* starring John Mills in the role of the British airman who avoids giving German interrogators information, based on the John Shore role. He had a fortnight's mystery assignment at Selfridges in 1944: it was a signals centre but we do not know what John's role there was. In January 1945 he was attached to No 30 military mission to Moscow, probably concerned with the repatriation of RAF PoWs caught by the Soviet advance westwards.

But then tragedy struck and John's wife Jo died in early 1947 aged only 29. Later that year John got remarried, to June Hadfield. In May 1948 they had John's third son, Ian. By then John had left the RAF temporarily but he re-joined in 1949. John worked with the Avro Lincoln bomber as a student at the RAF's Operational Conversion Unit (230 OCU). It was in Snowdonia on 15th March 1950, when flying this bomber on a night exercise, that John and his five crew were tragically killed: the navigator misheard a direction from the ground controller. John Shore was 32. He is buried, alongside Jo, in Battle Cemetery.

John Shore on return in 1942

EXTRACTS FROM THE DIARY OF THE CHIEF MEDICAL OFFICER: SIR ALAN MOORE, Bt, OF HANCOX, WHATLINGTON 1939-45

Compiled by Charlotte Moore; the bracketed commentaries in italics are also by her.

When the war began, Alan was Medical Officer of Health for the Battle district. He lived at Hancox with his wife Mary and their four children Norman, 16, a schoolboy at Eton, Hilary, 11, Richard, 8, and Meriel, 2. Hilary and Richard went daily to Caldbec House, Battle, where they shared a governess with Benedicta and Ralfe Whistler and some other local children.

1939

SEPT 3: By the wireless at 12 we learnt that we had been at war with Germany since 11.
To Watch Oak to inquire about a report of a sick refugee. Then back to the reception region [for evacuees]. To Emeleus' with a nurse for head soap....Policemen in steel helmets. Troops about. A small gun by the horse trough. To the reception area & the deanery for a mother & child.

SEPT 5: To Watch Oak. Much telephoning about emergency hospitals chiefly.
SEPT 6: Air raid warning about 5 to 7. All clear signal about 8.30.

SEPT 7: My car was prepared for night driving under the new regulations, at Watch Oak.

SEPT 14: Paid some visits in Battle in connexion with Evacuation.

Watch Oak today: HQ of Civil defence 1939-45

SEPT 15: Conference with billeting officers [at Watch Oak].
[*Alan was very busy at this time trying to establish emergency hospitals in the area, also with the evacuation programme*]

OCT 2: The Enumerator came in the evening & made out identification cards for everyone who was in the house on Friday night.

OCT 20: [*Departure of the "Quins", the five London schoolgirls who, with their teacher, had been evacuated to Hancox in August*].

DEC 5: The number of evacuated people in the Battle Rural District is 2015.

DEC 13: Soldiers pouring through Battle in khaki-coloured cars & motorcycles.

APR 30: No newspaper posters were displayed in Battle. We are being urged to save paper.

MAY 8: Rations for children of a second evacuation have arrived at Battle station.

MAY 10 Holland and Belgium invaded; gunfire heard at Hancox at lunchtime. At the Council Offices we had a telegram warning us to be ready for Dutch & Belgian refugees.

MAY 14 Tues: On Monday many soldiers were at Battle- Devonshire Territorials- some of the men very small. We owe their presence it is believed to fears of parachute troops being sent by the enemy, as in Holland & Belgium & elsewhere.

MAY 17: Barriers in North Trade Road & Upper Lake. Many military vehicles about.

MAY 18: Very grave news. The enemy has broken through the French line near Sedan. Hugh Whistler said that lorries full of troops were passing Caldbec House last night & returning empty, presumably having taken troops to Newhaven.

MAY 21: Noticed a machine gun post in Upper Lake, Battle, pointing as it might have been had it been Harold's.
While working at Battle school in the afternoon I was told that Dutch refugees had arrived at Rye harbour. [*Alan took his son Richard with him when he went to meet these refugees; see Richard's account*].

MAY 22: At the Council Offices I learnt that bombs had been dropped near Ticehurst [16 explosive bombs & 70 incendiary]. No one was killed but many chickens were.

MAY 26 SUNDAY: Last night I took duty in the control room from 9 to 9 this morning. The man on duty ordinarily has not much to do. He is there in case he is wanted. The 3 or 4 people in the Report Centre on the other side of the passage receive the messages & summon the necessary officers. At 11.15 we had a 'yellow' warning. Yellow signifies enemy aircraft are about- Col. Hume Spry (in charge of A.R.P.) soon arrived, & Mr Jenner (Chief Surveyor & Sanitary Inspector, Liaison Fire Brigade Officer) in his Fire Brigade uniform with a large buckle in front. Mr Bramley (in charge of water mains & sewers for repair party) arrived & Campany (Clerk to MDH & Chief Surveyor. Officer in charge of the report centre). These last two had not long left the building. Col.Sawyer [Sub controller & Commandant of 1st aid arrangements] arrived from Burwash.

Also came a police liaison officer in plain clothes; Field: the chief fire brigade officer; & later, an officer of the VI Devonshires.

After a time we could hear the aircrafts noise. Many search-lights swept the sky but clouds hid the enemy. Noise, & searchlights ceased but no 'white' message came which after a 'yellow' means finished & allows the officers specially summoned to go home.

We sat talking & drinking tea. Then came a message of a rumour of parachute troops dropped on the Winchelsea side of Rye & at Hawkins aerodrome near Dover. Col. Hume Spry reported this – I am not sure to whom besides the County subcontrol at Bexhill. After a time the rumour was confirmed from Lewes – parachutists dropped at Dover Folkestone & Rye Harbour.

Col. Hume-Spry asked for an armed guard which was soon forthcoming & orders were given to the soldiers to close the barricades. An armed guard was also asked for the fire stations at Icklesham & Camber at each of which only one man was on duty. The Fire Brigade officer pointed out how easy it would be for the enemy to overpower these men & drive away with the fire engines & so get about the country unsuspected for a long time. Near Icklesham fire station is an automatic telephone exchange. No report of parachute troops being seen on the ground was received, but though the white signal came at last people remained on duty until daylight. I went to bed at half past 4. Col. Hume Spry relieved me at 9. Old cars & other stuff were ready to put across the road at the bottom of the Watch Oak drive but were not actually in position.

Leaders of the Civil Defence in Battle 1939-45
Front from left : Miss Alfari; Mrs Hewett; Col Hume-Spry; unknown; Betty Whatley(?)
Rear from left: H G Seymour; Mr Nash; Mr C R Stavert; George Bramley; unknown

Many "yellow" reports have been received recently, as many as 5 in a week. This means little sleep for the officers who have to turn out.

MAY 27: The landing of parachutists has not been confirmed. It is thought the parachutes may have carried magnetic mines.

JUNE 2: This morning after early service [at Whatlington church] Col. Wilson showed me where it was proposed to bury the chalice & patten. Only Mr Browell [clergyman] Col. Wilson and I are to know.

JUNE 5:Twenty military vehicles passed between the bottom of Riccard's

Lane & Caldbec Hill. All signposts were gone & dis-armed.

JUNE 8: Last night June 7-8 I went on duty in the control room at 9. At 2.32 we had a 'yellow' message. Col. Hume Spry & others came. The 'white' message came in about 20 minutes. Col. H-S had just gone home & had put his car away when a second 'yellow' came at 3.10. We heard that the German plane or planes had gone along the coast. Great concrete pipes filled with cement are taking the place of the old waggons etc at the barricades. These pipes are made by a factory at Rye Harbour. This afternoon I bathed at Glyne Gap & found all the coast fortified. There are square wooden frames being sunk in the shingle to serve I suppose as pits for riflemen.

I am told that cattle are being taken from Romney Marsh, & that some bridges near have been demolished.

All foreigners are being interned or moved. Questier the Belgian settler at Whatlington after the last war, has had to go.

JUNE 10: Today I was given a civilian duty pass.

JUNE 11: On the Robertsbridge road near Battle I, going towards Robertsbridge, passed about 6 queer military vehicles with caterpillar apparatus instead of ordinary wheels. The men hardly showed. They were going towards Robertsbridge.

JUNE 12: I passed three howitzers going through Battle.

JUNE 13: I learnt later they were Bren carriers.

JUNE 14: The news is frightful, Paris all but taken & perhaps Havre.

JUNE 20: [*Alan and his wife Mary decide to send their younger children to relations in Somerset*]. We don't feel sure that it is safer, but we fear a sudden ordered evacuation of these parts in which they might be sent somewhere where we knew no one.

JULY 7: Nearly all the south coast has been declared a 'defence area'. We are waiting.

[*Many bombs in the area in this period: explosions shake the house*]

JULY 26: I met Mr Jenner our chief surveyor & then Mr Francis a sanitary inspector & later Dr Maxwell. From these & others I learnt that bombs had fallen near Pean's Wood (House), about 200 yards from Maxwell's house, also near Willards Hill.

Mr Francis heard a screaming bomb that fell near Guestling. The German machine was chased off by two of ours & people at Battle heard machine gun fire & went out to look.

JULY 29: A German plane came down of its own accord at Buckholt near Catsfield. It had not dropped its bombs. Its crew went to sleep almost directly they were captured.

There has been a good deal of fighting in the air near here just lately.

[*Alan and Mary Moore decide that their children should return home from Somerset*]

AUGUST 5: The air raid siren went at the Battle Council Offices about 11.45 p.m. I heard & some people saw a plane fly over in a direction W of N. The all clear siren sounded in about 20 minutes. People who man (& woman) the mobile first-aid post & who come for other purposes arrived commendably quickly.

AUGUST 7: I have just filled in the enrolment form for the Home Guard.

AUGUST 15: Air raid warnings in the morning & afternoon...we could see from just outside the District Council offices at Battle 4 or 5 aeroplanes flying very high. One kept turning & seemed to be attacking one of the others & I should feel no doubt of it if it were not for the fact that we heard no sound of machine-gun fire. This may have been because they were down wind as well as very high up.

AUGUST 19: Yesterday Benedicta & Ralfe Whistler came to picnic with Hilary & Richard. They had to be recalled from the fields to the garden because the air raid siren sounded about 5 to 1. Later the exhausts of aircraft could be seen overhead & some of us saw them dodging about showing that fighting was going on. The children had to come indoors.

[Civilians killed at Rye] I learnt also today that a German airman had died in Rye Hospital at Playden. He was greatly smashed. I was told he would have a military funeral with a swastika flag.

AUGUST 22: Met Sheppard [Battle solicitor] at Battle who told me that there was a truculent prisoner at the Abbey who said 'I refuse to speak to anyone but an officer & he must be in uniform'. Offered a newspaper he refused, saying English newspapers were all lies. He said also that the Germans would be at the Abbey in three weeks.

Sunday AUGUST 25: Yesterday I learnt that on Friday night the first casualties in the Battle Rural District occurred; two people injured near Burwash.
Air raid warnings are now so frequent that I don't record them.

German maps have been found in hides in the woods of Brightling Park. On August 23 I met Tew [owner of Brightling Park] outside the Battle Council Offices & mentioned them. He told me he had found another & had just taken it to the Police. It was of Baltic countries.

AUGUST 27: Last night I was woken by planes & learnt that they had been passing all night to a great attack on London.

AUGUST 30: At Ticehurst this morning examining children at Coronation Cottages for going to Canada, and a fierce battle developed overhead. The woman of the house told me that a few days ago she was thrown out of bed by a bomb's explosion. We had glimpses of planes & could hear some diving to the attack. Machine gun fire was frequent & there were four or five bumps, no doubt bombs. We heard also what sounded like two rifle shots. A soldier on sick leave & a man in a leather peaked cap & I stood together & shared my glasses [*binoculars*]. Much the same sort of thing was to be seen from Battle yesterday.

SEPT 5: Yesterday I had my first exercise with the Home Guard. About a dozen mustered at the observation post in the New Road [A21- the post was on the left hand side of the road in the Hastings direction, about a quarter of a mile south of Hancox], Col.King of Sedlescombe in charge of operations. Two of us were not in uniform. I had my LDV armlet. I brought my gun. Someone, I think a regular, went off with a flag. He represented a body of the enemy. We had to try & get within 50 yards or so. We had an exercise on each side of the road. We straggled & talked too much & were inclined not to get into a proper line for firing.

SEPT 6: An air battle overhead between 9.30 and 10 this morning. We could see many planes very high up & hear violent machine gun fire. Presently a plane roared overhead. Richard said he saw a man in it & that it seemed near our chimneys. I did not see it till it was some way off towards Hastings. Norman said smoke was coming from it & that it was a German. It was pursued by one of our planes. I learnt later that a German came down in the sea near Pett.
Last night about 500 incendiary bombs were dropped in a pine wood near The Squirrel at Ashburnham...2 or 3 planes both British & German came down yesterday & to-day in or near the Battle R.D.

SEPT 11: Norman near the reservoir east of Sedlescombe saw an air battle. He saw 60 or 70 German planes. One bomber came low over the trees & English fighters dived repeatedly on it. There was a great explosion not far off. I saw it from Watch Oak Battle & so did Richard from Caldbec House. Mary & Hilary were hop-picking at Great Knelle & saw the same fight. At 6 the Prime Minister spoke in the wireless of the recent indiscriminate bombing of London & told us that the enemy was preparing to invade us from Norway to Bordeaux.

SEPT 13: Yesterday Hilary & Richard went with the Whistler children to see where the plane that flew so near Norman & blew up, had come down. They brought back small pieces of metal: part of a leather cap & a bullet...The plane had a crew of 5. When our Home Guard ran up, three Germans came towards them crying 'bombs, bombs'. Asked, they said one dead man & one wounded man was in the plane. Before our people could get nearer to rescue him the bombs exploded. Mr Bramley told me that one of the engines, more than a man could lift, was hurled about 100 yards.

One body was fairly whole & one in bits. They were taken to Battle Abbey. Lusty, acting Clerk to the Rural District Council, was kept busy arranging their burial.
[*Elphick, owner of Whatlington garage, said a bomb fell nearby at 3 a.m.*]
Norman, Hilary & I have just been to Elphick's. Sure enough in the midst of a green field on the opposite hill to the right of Wood's Place is a circular brown patch. Evidently the railway was aimed at. Considering how few anti-aircraft guns there are in these parts the enemy should have done better. I think one of our planes would have.
Hilary [aged 12] said how dull it would be when the war was over.

SEPT 18: Several incendiaries fell near the Battle end of the Marley Lane & H.E (H*igh Explosive*) bombs near the tannery [where Tesco garage now is].

SEPT 19 Huge bomb near Brightling: the largest yet fallen in this county.

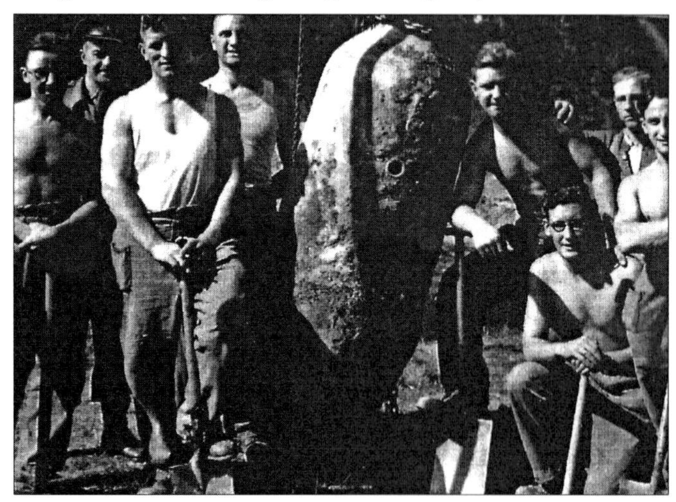

Bomb disposal squad in 1946, stationed at Burntwood, Powdermill Lane
Third from left Frank Finch, then Corporal Gage and George Wickenden

SEPT 25: Joan Whistler told me that there was another loud explosion last night...Hugh Whistler saw the tracer bullets being fired...bomber brought down near Ore church. I had passed the fire engine hurrying through Battle.

SEPT 27: Hugh Whistler told me he saw a barrage balloon adrift this morning & that it was set on fire by a plane.

SEPT 28: [*Norman, on Home Guard duty, found a fragment of an English map of Birmingham and district in a field*] I took it to the Police in case certain marks in red should have been added by the enemy & should denote points in our defences.
...7 bombs dropped about NNW perhaps half a mile from the Watch Oak. No damage was done.
...During lunch a great air battle was fought overhead, but cumulus cloud prevented our seeing much. We saw a squadron of what Norman thought were Messerschmidts flying in 3 groups of 3. We heard the sound of diving attacks & of machine gun fire.

SEPT 30: Mary & Norman were shot at by a bomber that came low while they were walking in the old green coach road between Ashburnham Park & Netherfield. They had to hide under a hedge.

OCT 4: A bomb that fell near Richard's Hill & broke the Frasers' windows [in Powdermill Lane] shook the Battle Council Offices.

OCT 19: Today I saw a man I know, Bishop, in Battle with a crutch. He told me that a fortnight ago having just got out of a taxi by the War Office [in London]...the driver & cab were suddenly blown to pieces...He woke to find himself on the sandwich bar of an eating house bleeding badly from a foot.

OCT 20 [*a German plane chasing an army lorry was flying low over the drive at Hancox, firing bullets*]

OCT 27 [*much air fighting all week*] The VI Devons are leaving Battle shortly. Yesterday Richard & I saw what we were told was a Retreat in front of the Abbey gateway. There was a band & a bugle & drum band which marched & countermarched and a few men with rifles & helmets for inspection. They marched in & out- perhaps 7 different men appeared- of the Abbey gateway & the gates were opened & shut. The low sun shone on the building within the gate. At the end the regimental colour was lowered from the flagstaff outside the gate & after 'Abide with me' & 'God save the King' they marched in to another tune & the gates were shut. Dusk had fallen.

NOV 17: Air raid warnings are very frequent. 1001 High Explosive bombs have fallen in the Battle Rural District of 33 parishes with a normal population of about 30,000. No civilians have been killed. About 15 have been wounded, 5 I believe seriously. The first bomb fell on May 22. I have not had access to military casualty lists but am told that 2 or 3 soldiers have been killed. [*NB outside the Battle Rural District civilians had been killed, in Rye, Hastings, and Eastbourne*].

NOV 21: [*description of immunising the children living in St Clement's Caves in Hastings*]

DEC 9: Today a lecturer came to the Council offices from London. He came by road because of damage last night to the Railway. He said that London Bridge was damaged, so London Bridge is broken down, or almost again- was not the last time before the days of King Alfred? The lecturer said the BBC had been hit. We are however getting the news today.

DEC 22: Norman & I went to the Sedlescombe hall for the Home Guard drill. We were taken out & it was explained how we should hold the line of the Brede channel. This we gathered would actually be the Home Guard's job- about 40 of us, not all with rifles.

DEC 23: Today I learnt in the control room that a German bomber was brought down in flames at Etchingham. It was hit by anti-aircraft guns over Pevensey levels. Some of the crew may be at large. It was a Heinkel III (cxi) tho' the wireless said it was a Junkers. Three men were killed & one made prisoner.

DEC 30: Yesterday evening coming out of church about half past 7 saw a glare in the NW. To-day we learnt that many fire bombs were dropped on London.

1941

JAN 6: We are all thinking about the invasion of this country.

JAN 20: A conference of Military officers or something of the kind was held at Battle Abbey this morning. I took four officers to it from Caldbec Hill. Their car had broken down.

JAN 22: An iron sentrybox-like structure has appeared on the roof of the District Council Offices. It is for the fire-watcher.

I learnt that Battle, Robertsbridge, Northiam & Winchelsea were to be held as 'nodal points'.

At Battle, perhaps at all, there are the outer defences of barbed wire, the inner defences of concrete 'dragons'-teeth' & the keep. I don't know where the last is to be.

"Dragon's teeth" (anti - tank traps) around Battle Abbey and the Deanery

JAN 26: At Home Guard exercise to-day Col. King told us that the enemy were known to have ready, besides their flat-bottomed craft for invasion, 4 divisions of 'crash landing' troops to be brought by air. Such divisions consist of 8000 men each.

JAN 27: Mr Francis returned to duty at the Council Offices after a fortnight's course at Falfield near Bristol. He was told that the Germans certainly intend to use gas, probably mustard gas chiefly.

JAN 28: Noticed pairs of sandbags (I suppose that is what they are) near houses. Counted 25 pair between Hancox & Caldbec House. Most of them were by telegraph poles.

JAN 31: About 3.40 I was at Watch Oak & heard an explosion that shook the building.
[*'Alerts' were frequent at this time*].

FEB 6: One of our Councillors Fry who is in our fire brigade went to Portsmouth after the recent severe bombing. He said that parties of firemen came from pretty well every borough south of Birmingham. He believed that Battle Rural District was the only rural district which sent help.

FEB 9: This morning from 9.30 to 12.30 the Home Guard had exercises with regulars. We were supposed to be holding a part of the line of the Brede against parachute troops. The pretended enemy were distinguished by white squares on their helmets & these gave some measure of the way in which khaki blends with country surroundings. Often I am sure we should not have seen the troops had it not been for the patches of white.

FEB 15: A stream of lorries & light-guns perhaps anti-aircraft poured from Battle to Whatlington this afternoon. Richard who had to hide in the hedge, on his bicycle, to avoid a swerving lorry said he had heard there were manoeuvres lasting 3 days.

FEB 16: [*new rifles issued to Home Guard*] a new pattern, 300 bore instead of 303 were issued with bayonets & 30 rounds with each. Only 10 were allowed to Section IV, Whatlington.

FEB 24: There is an anti-aircraft gun in the field opposite Caldbec House. Fresh troops have replaced those lately in this region.

I met Questier who being foreign had to go to Reigate.[see June 8 1940]. He said he was quite comfortable. I gathered that he lived there like an ordinary inhabitant.

MAR 5: A battalion of the Lancashire Fusiliers are now at Vine Hall & Home Place.

MAR 20: On March 19 we were woke by an explosion. Later I heard that several bombs had fallen at Crowhurst. One fell near a cottage & killed the man within. He & his wife were buried. His death is the first death of a civilian caused by the enemy's air activity in the 33 parishes of the Battle District.

[*This evening*] the air war full of the growling of planes...a heavy attack on London...many bombs fell near Etchingham. it was a glorious starry night.

MAR 31: Many Army cars & lorries & Bren gun carriers about especially between Battle & Whatlington just after 5.

APR 2: Many army vehicles of all sorts between Battle & Hurst Green.

APR 5: It appeared that the many Army lorries etc were engaged in manoeuvres.

APR 14: A large gun passed through Battle to-day drawn by a lorry.

The Battle District subscribed more than £ 135,000 in War Weapons Week.

APR 15: The manager of the Battle Westminster Bank told me that to prevent inflation no overdrafts for private purposes were to be allowed. This is very serious for us & may mean our taking Norman from Cambridge. [*It didn't!*]

APR 24: I was told in the Control Room a German plane was brought down on Camber golf links & another into the sea, at 8.30.

MAY 4, SUNDAY: We had an exercise at Battle as though the barriers were closed. I was stationed at the Almonry, a casualty- receiving station in charge of Dr. Davidson.
On the whole military & civil arrangements seem to work well.

MAY 12: Today seeing a middle-aged woman & a youth with hand luggage walking towards Whatlington about 1/4 a mile from Caldbec Hill I offered them a lift. They were from Liverpool where their house had been bombed. 'There's nothing but blitz in Liverpool' said the woman. Her other son was stationed at Battle which was why they had come. I had just left an old coat of Norman's at the WVS Headquarters for the boy about whom Mary had heard that he had no clothes but what he stood in.

MAY 16: Today I drew my Home Guard rifle a 300 bore Eddystone 1917, an American make I believe; also 45 rounds of ammunition.
My action station is at Battle in a medical capacity, but I am allowed to go in the Home Guard in case I might be useful. I might not be able to get to Battle.

JUNE 5: To-day I was on duty for roof watching at the Battle Council Offices.
About 10 to 1 the siren sounded.
Someone relieved me about 20 minutes later to let me have my lunch & 20 minutes after that the all clear sounded.

JUNE 14: I was woke by 2 bumps. Learnt later that a German plane was brought down near to Snailham. Mr Spence the Fire Brigade chief told me he took a German prisoner. Part of a field of oats or wheat was burned.
We have had no porridge for nearly a week.

JUNE 22: Norman & I learnt from Mr Browell [*Rector of Whatlington*] as we were going to Church early that Germany had declared war on Russia.

JUNE 30: A little after 6 pm. Many planes are overhead going about SW. I counted 20 at least in the first flight, fighters I think. Mrs Elphick of Whatlington garage counted 80 & at 7, planes were still coming over. The siren sounded about 7. Before this distant explosions could be heard. Wind about SW.

JULY 7: No marmalade at breakfast. This brings home the war.
In the afternoon I examined all the children at Rye Harbour, 80, in case they should have to be moved suddenly.

AUG 7: The roads are occupied by troops, tanks & other military machines & aeroplanes flying low. When I got home for lunch I found the drive almost blocked. Our squatters are Scots Guards. They represent the enemy.

SEPT 9: [*returning home by train from Brighton*] At the ticket barrier a Naval CPO greeted me &...told me he was the first man to be called up from Battle where he had been in the Post Office.

SEPT 19: Stakes wholly whitened or with white heads have been set up at perhaps 20 yard intervals by many roads as guides at night.

OCT 25: Yesterday at 8 in the evening a meeting was held in our drawing room to which Carter the Territorial Army Commandant came to discuss measures to be taken in the event of an invasion. Thirteen people were present, the Police Sgt, Mr Hunt the chief warden, Lane in command of the Home Guard among them.
The chief points discussed were food dumps, dealing with casualties, disposal of the dead, an information centre, not using the roads or the telephone.
The County is being repeatedly warned that the Enemy intends invasion when he shall have beaten Russia.

NOV 26: We see many troops & lorries & the like but the county is much quieter than in peacetime.

DEC 11: From Battle I saw a barrage balloon that was adrift. I was on fire watching duty to-day at the Council Offices.

DEC 13: Norman went to Battle & registered. We hope he will be allowed to stay at Cambridge & take his degree which he can do at the end of his second year. He is training as a gunner & has Certificate B.

DEC 21: Since now I have duties in the Civil Defence casualty service & the First Aid Commandant is not a Medical man & my action station would be at Battle, I to-day took a letter to Lane the sergeant of my section or whatever it is tendering my resignation from the Home Guard.

1942

JAN 1: This afternoon coming down the slope from the Council Offices I found a short stout man in a blue jersey under his coat discussing with a middle-aged woman what had been happening. I joined the conversation & was told that a Hastings fishing-boat had been sunk (or burnt) & a man in her: 'an old pal of his' said the woman- was killed. His name was Philips.

JAN 15: Yesterday at the Royal East Sussex Hospital [*Hastings*] the Matron told of the fear some wounded German airmen had been in. They had been told they would be ill-treated if taken prisoner.
They said they were sent to attack Hastings for practice because it was so easy to find with its two piers.
This morning I attended a conference at the District Council offices on matters arising out of a probable alteration in the boundaries of the area that is to be defended. Soldiers, Councillors, Officials, Police & others were present.

MAR 29: It is plain that the crisis of the war is approaching.

APR 12: On Sunday the Home Guard, Norman among them, went to Whatlington Church in the evening & also RAF Cadets from Battle.

APR 16: Being on fire-watching duty at the DC Offices I had to go on the roof when the air-raid siren sounded about half past four. The all clear bell which warns the watcher to come down was rung in 5 or 10 minutes.

MAY 18: Several tanks, making a great noise, passed through Battle in the afternoon, about 2, going towards Robertsbridge. They seemed very large. There may have been a dozen.

JUNE 2: Fighter planes -I was told about 50 - flew low over Battle about 10.30 a.m. going about South.

JUNE 10: A way has been made through the barbed wire East of the De La Warr Pavilion allowing people to get on to the beach for bathing. I walked down & put my hand in the sea.

JUNE 14: To-day was set apart for re-affirming the unity of the nations allied against Germany & the rest. As head of the casualty services I attended Battle Church. The service began at 11. At it were Canadian troops RAF cadets Civil Defence workers & others. The lesson was well read by a Canadian officer. Kipling's Recessional, quite unsuitably, was one of the hymns. Afterwards to the Green where a platform had been set up to its right side towards the Abbey. On this heads of departments & others had seats. Hugh Whistler read out a message from the Prime Minister. Then the troops & others headed by a drum & bugle band marched past saluting at the platform. The troops & RAF cadets marched particularly well.

JULY 29: A great military exercise is going on. The Army is everywhere. 200 military vehicles have been in the Forestall [*the front field at Hancox*]. [*Several Army officers slept on the floor at Hancox*].
[*In September there was much bombing of the coastal towns and Rye*].

OCT 1: [*Norman went to train at Warley barracks in Essex*]

OCT 6: Yesterday evening the house was shaken several times by explosions. Twice they opened the drawing room door.

OCT 24: One of our planes came down at Netherfield. The pilot was killed.

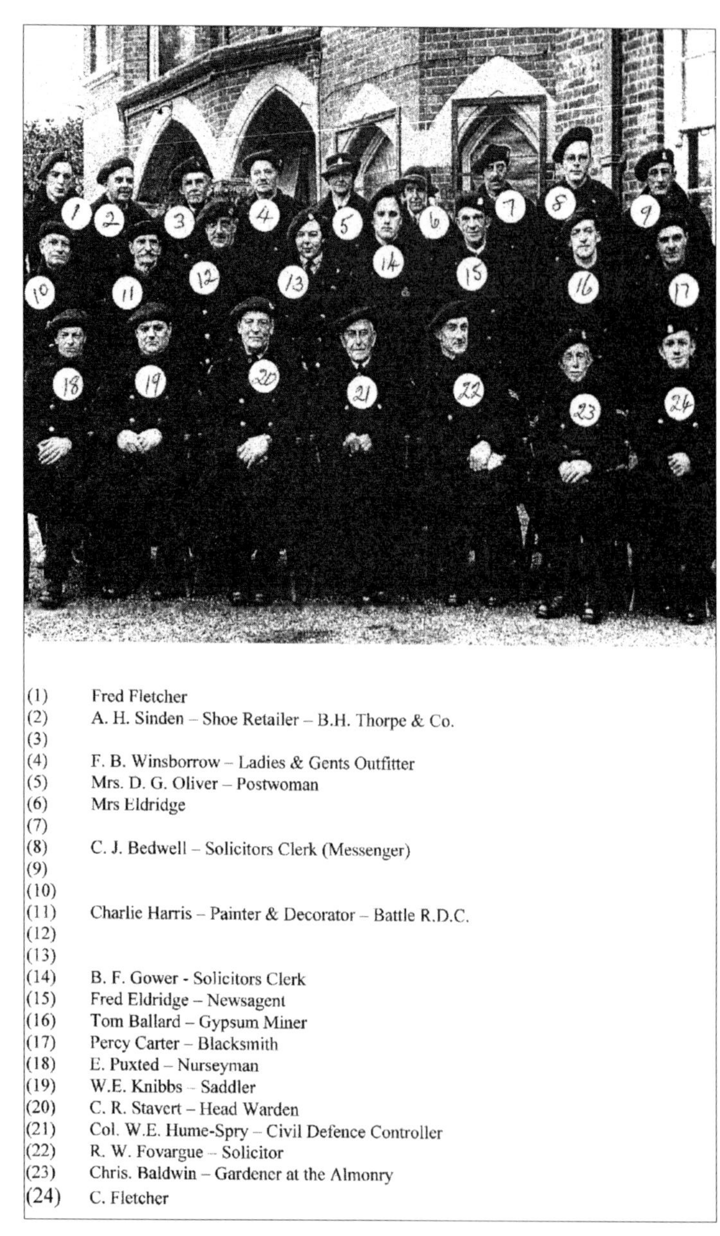

(1) Fred Fletcher
(2) A. H. Sinden – Shoe Retailer – B.H. Thorpe & Co.
(3)
(4) F. B. Winsborrow – Ladies & Gents Outfitter
(5) Mrs. D. G. Oliver – Postwoman
(6) Mrs Eldridge
(7)
(8) C. J. Bedwell – Solicitors Clerk (Messenger)
(9)
(10)
(11) Charlie Harris – Painter & Decorator – Battle R.D.C.
(12)
(13)
(14) B. F. Gower - Solicitors Clerk
(15) Fred Eldridge – Newsagent
(16) Tom Ballard – Gypsum Miner
(17) Percy Carter – Blacksmith
(18) E. Puxted – Nurseyman
(19) W.E. Knibbs – Saddler
(20) C. R. Stavert – Head Warden
(21) Col. W.E. Hume-Spry – Civil Defence Controller
(22) R. W. Fovargue – Solicitor
(23) Chris. Baldwin – Gardener at the Almonry
(24) C. Fletcher

Civil Defence Wardens 1945-46

OCT 26: At 1 loud reports almost like thunder were heard at Battle.

NOV 8: [*victory in Egypt*] Everyone is cheered by some success at last & is encouraged to feel that the tide of war has turned.

NOV 15: The church bells rang this evening [*for victory in Egypt*]. Meriel [*aged nearly 7*] was thrilled.

DEC 16: We heard gunfire from Battle & was [*sic*] told that our guns had been firing at one of our planes that was flying too low, somewhere between Powder Mill Lane & Crowhurst.

DEC 22: Driving home to lunch, in Mount St I saw a soldier with luggage. I slowed & offered him a lift & it was Norman! He has finished at Wrotham pre O.C.T.U [*Officer Cadet Training Units*]. & after Xmas is to go to an O.C.T.U. at Ilkley in Yorkshire.

DEC 24: On fire watching duty at the Council Offices. The siren sounded about 4 & I was on the roof about 20 minutes.

1943

JAN 4: About 5 to 1 loud explosions were heard at Battle...I learnt that bombs had been dropped at Winchelsea Beach...The plane, a Fokker-Wolf was shot down & its crew of one killed.

JAN 21: [*big raid on Jan 20*] a man was somewhat hurt at Ashburnham in yesterday's raid but no one else in the Battle district.

JAN 28: About 20 to 12 3 German planes flew low over the District Council offices. I heard them & wondered whose they were. Some people saw them & the crosses on them. Quite soon followed two heavy explosions, perhaps 3. Hastings gas works at Bulverhythe were hit.

FEB 2: At 10 to 9 while at breakfast planes could be heard. Then the house was shaken by an explosion quickly followed by another. Then the siren sounded. Before leaving for Rye to attend a meeting to discuss plans for dealing with invasion...we heard that Battle had been bombed.

In the afternoon I went to Battle. I didn't see any damage on the way to the Council Offices except that the windows of the Towers Hotel were broken.
In the High St, Tickner's shop near the Green had been hit & the proprietors Mr & Mrs Giles killed. Behind the shop was a mass of wreckage, many buildings had fallen. Joan Whistler who saw the bomb fall from Caldbec House said it looked as though most of the High St had gone up. Twelve people were hurt or shocked * (*two more reported today 3/2/43) One bomb bounced through the Abbey gate & broke to pieces without exploding. I saw the bits lying just outside the gateway. Many windows in High St were broken. Another bomb burst somewhere to the West quite near. Planes or a plane fired at Westfield & in Kent Street wounding 2 people at Westfield & one at Kent St.

FEB 9: Our Times did not come. Inquiring at Wiltons in Sedlescombe I was told it had been delayed by some activity of the enemy on the railway.

FEB 15: [*deaths at Rye*] The Council stood in silence in honour of those who had lost their lives.

APR 20: It is announced that Church bells may be rung on Sunday in future.

MAY 24: [*heavy raid on Hastings*]

JUNE 5: I was on duty with Miss Whatley, my clerk, in the Reports Centre at the Battle Council Offices. No warning came. Mr Churchill we learnt this morning is back in England. Everyone is wondering where the Allies will strike their greatest blows.

JUNE 13: Richard, Meriel & I drove to Battle & met Norman about ten this morning. He was in 2nd Lieutenant's uniform....Norman says that he has been taught that the great difference in measures against the enemy in this war & the last is the enormously more powerful explosives now used.

JULY 10:Many planes were heard this morning. Some made an unfamiliar sound. I had meant to note...that we were expecting for news of great doings any day & to-day we learn that we have invaded Sicily. There has been heavy fighting on the Russian front for several days.

AUG 11: Mr Hunt our local [*blank in MS*] telephoned after tea to-day that anti-personnel bombs had been dropped in this region. He asked that the W.V.S. & anyone else should be informed.
...There is a feeling of great events impending. The Prime Minister is in Canada.

AUG 14: This afternoon I relieved Col. Sawyer standing by near Woodlands farm, west of Burwash while the military & the police searched for bombs. We had to lie down in a field quite a long way off while 4 or 5 that had been found were exploded.

SEPT 3: Four years ago we went to war with Germany. At 11 many of the staff at the Council Office staff gathered in the hall & listened to a short broadcast service.

We have learnt to-day that the Allies have landed in Italy.

At 7 in the evening there was a short open air service in Mountfield Cricket Ground. We all went with Rose Smith [*servant at Hancox*] in our car. Norman & Hilary & Margaret Baker [*servant at Hancox*] bicycled. There had been a service in the hop garden at Hancox in the morning.

SEPT 18: News of the unconditional surrender of Italy! Norman & I were told in a bus from Hastings to Battle.

OCT 17: *[bomb near Crowhurst*]

OCT 18: 4 people were killed by the bomb at Crowhurst & 16 hurt of whom 4 were sent to Hospital. A bomb fell also at Dallington.

OCT 19: I had to go this afternoon to Crowhurst to see if a cottage damaged by the bomb last Sunday were habitable by a large family. It was not. The family had been bombed in London. Luckily an empty cottage was found.

OCT 22: We were woken at a quarter past 3 by a bomb that shook the house. We learnt it had fallen at Battle Barn Farm.

OCT 22: No, it was Beauford Farm up a farm road next beyond the Marley Lane, going towards Hastings. Mary & I visited it this afternoon. The pit made by the bomb was about 30 feet across & looked 10 or 12 ft deep.

DEC 2: At tea time soldiers were all about Hancox - some sort of manoeuvres we think are going on. We are putting up two officers. Riccards Lane was blocked with military vehicles.

1944

JAN 22: 16 High Explosive bombs & innumerable incendiaries fell in the Battle District & there was not a single casualty.

FEB 19: During the morning signposts reappeared.

FEB 23: the new German pilotless radio-directed aeroplane & the rocket gun...

APR 20: Yesterday in a field behind & above Home Place I found two incendiary bombs sticking into the ground at an acute angle. I went to Home place & 2 soldiers came with me & picked them up. The bombs may have been 18" long & 3" in diameter.
The secrets of our impending attack on the Continent are well kept.

MAY 1: I was asked by the Battle market for my identity card by a policeman. I had left it in the car. The policeman said Battle was now a military area.

MAY 3: I got a new identity card from the Food Office at Battle. It reads that I am engaged in Civil Defence.

MAY 9: It is just past full moon. We are expecting our great attack on the enemy to begin when the dark nights come.

MAY 12: Battle High Street in the afternoon was lined with soldiers. A Military Policeman at the top of Riccard's Lane told me that Mr Churchill & the Dominion Premiers were visiting. [*They would have visited Northiam earlier in the day to review troops: there are commemorative plaques there. They would then have gone through Battle to reach the coast, perhaps to review defences.*]

MAY 30: An air raid warning about 2.39 a.m. Mary is standing by to go away for a week to do something connected with the war. We do not know what. Yesterday we gave a Lieut. Jarvis stationed at Cripps's Corner a bath & his batman one too. We had to refuse giving 20 a week from shortage of water.

Churchill , Smuts and the other Commonwealth leaders
(Fraser of New Zealand, Curtin of Australia, King of Canada) 1944

JUNE 3: We are all wondering when the great attack will begin. The Moon is getting on towards full.

JUNE 6: We were woken by planes which seemed unusually low. Three or four minutes past 5 a.m. the house was shaken by an explosion which was evidently severe & not far off. Perhaps a quarter of an hour later there was another not quite so heavy. Before we got up May Buckwell [cook at Hancox] came & told us that a plane had come down at the foot of Caldbec Hill & that the ordinary road to Battle was not allowed. I had

to go to Battle by the Marley Lane. I learnt that it had been announced that we had landed in France. I was told that a Teacher at Battle School had said that there were many craft off Hastings. The 'plane that came down was American. I went to see it in the afternoon. It was burnt to pieces. All the crew but one were killed. Another I learnt came down at Ashburnham & another at Ninfield: the cause was a collision. An American army lorry gave me a lift as far as the road barrier going towards Whatlington. It went on & so did I on foot & just beyond the gate of Ringletts [farm in Whatlington Road] saw 2 holes perhaps 18" across in the road. I was told 10 bombs ad fallen. I saw 2 more holes in a field on the same side of the road as Ringletts. You could see down about 5 ft, then there was earth. I was told the holes were 20 ft deep.
...Mrs Arnould of the W.V.S. tel'd & asked Mary to be ready to go at 9 a.m. tomorrow to a place unknown for a week...We guess it is to help in a camp for French refugees.
Yesterday 2 soldiers came & had baths.

JUNE 7: *[Mary was sent to a camp at Sompting]*

JUNE 16: ...radio-directed 'planes were sent over by the enemy.

JUNE 18: More radio-directed 'planes last night. We could see a bright light & beautiful red lights like the stars of Roman Candles. These I'm told are tracer bullets.

JUNE 22: Life is punctuated by explosions. I saw a flying torpedo - they are not radio-directed- shot down on June 20. Yesterday I went to the Duke's Wood [beyond Leeford Place in Whatlington] on this side of the line where one had exploded. It was as though there was a patch of winter in the wood, the leaves being all stript off. Small fragments of the machine lay about.

JUNE 28: 61 flying torpedoes have been brought down in the Battle District. Two people, one an Italian prisoner, were killed by one while ploughing at Poppinghole Farm [near Robertsbridge] to-day.

JULY 7: [*Flying torpedo brings down plaster at Hancox*]

JULY 11: Several houses damaged near the railway bridge at Whatlington. The WVS mobile canteen not being available we & Mrs Thompson took tea, made at Leeford Farm, to the men at repair work.

JULY 20: 14 [torpedoes] before 1 a.m.

JULY 30: The most prominent feature of the war for us in S. England are the flying torpedoes- crewless aeroplanes which are sent over every day & every night.
The weather which has been unusually cloudy since the beginning of June has favoured them. They are chased by our planes & we often hear gunfire & then a bump. Sometimes the house is shaken severely.

JULY 31: The Billeting Officer at Battle learnt from the Ministry at 11 this morning that mothers & children must be examined today, for going away tomorrow . Miss Ingram of the WVS drove me in the afternoon from Watch Oak to the Battle Church Hall [& then on to other towns & villages- a round trip of 55 miles]. We passed many damaged houses.

AUG 3: ...unusually large number of bombs...

AUG 4: Driving from Rye to Battle this afternoon...on the Rye side of Cripps's Corner I heard gunfire & saw people taking shelter. I stopped & saw roughly to the W perhaps NW a flying torpedo chased by one of our planes which was firing at it. The torpedo exploded & the report took a surprisingly long time to be heard where I was, 5 seconds, perhaps. It was smart.
When I got to Watch Oak I found the stained glass window had been damaged, frame & glass. There was some plaster down in some of the rooms, a few flakes of something only in mine. One clerk had a finger cut by glass.

AUG 6: Mary, Hilary, Richard & Meriel going to Whatlington church met [*Malcolm*] Muggeridge who is in Military Intelligence. He said that the allies might be in Paris soon & thought that the end of the war was near... Evidently he thinks that the Germans are going to collapse soon.

AUG 9: Miss Ingram of the WVS...told me that 5000 houses & buildings had been damaged in the Battle district. I don't know whether a farm house & its cart lodge would count as 2.

AUG 12: [*Norman on leave*] We do not know whence he has gone. He looked very well & is confident of victory...he said that it was thought the war, apart from the Japanese, might be over before Christmas.
About 11 pm a flying bomb exploded, it seemed just overhead. We had several windows broken & plaster down. Mary, Hilary & Richard got up & went to the Woodgates at the cottage at the top of Stream Lane to see if anyone was hurt or needed shelter.

AUG 13 [*damage to Whatlington Church*]
In the morning with commendable promptitude Mr, Bramley the Works Engineer of the District Council who is in charge of repairs, came & noted our damage. [*damage to house, outbuildings and neighbouring cottages].*

AUG 15: When I got home to tea I found men at work making temporary repairs of our damage of Aug 12.

AUG 23: I learnt at the Council Offices that the bomb at 6.20 that morning had fallen near Marley Lane.
Coming home just before 1 I overtook several large guns (4-inch?) towed by things like enormous vans. There were also things being towed that I could not recognise.

AUG 30: Yesterday 22 flying bombs were shot down in the Battle district, the highest number yet in one day.

SEPT 3: [*5th anniversary of war*] Victory seems to be in sight. [Allies in Belgium; surrender of Finland]. We all went to Whatlington Church for the half-past six service, a special service. The Home Guard was present & occupied almost all the right side of the Church.

Sept 5 [*Hilary and Benedicta Whistler going to Gloucestershire to do land work*].

SEPT 7: Mr Bramley the Works Engineer told me that 1384 ordinary bombs & 412 flying bombs had been shot down in the Battle district. Fire watching is no longer required in full & in some places the blackout restrictions are to be much reduced.[*Not in Battle*]

SEPT 10 In the Times -yesterday's- was a statement that of the places on the way to London most flying bombs had come down at Ashford in Kent & that Tunbridge Wells & the Battle district were equal for second place. It is peaceful not having them.

SEPT 13 [*trees blasted by bombs put forth new foliage as in spring. Oak, ash & alder.]*

SEPT 17 [*blackout relaxed to 'dim-out'*]

OCT 19: Ordinary petrol pumps are soon to be allowed to supply petrol.

OCT 30: The Home Guard though not abolished is to cease being active.

NOV 6: The Prime Minister has told the country not to expect the defeat of the enemy before the spring or early summer.

NOV 12: The enemy is sending rocket bombs which are said to go 60 or 70 miles high.
[*In November, Norman was overseas, first in Belgium and then in Holland*].

NOV 20: Mary & Meriel found the barbed wire & other discouragements to invaders gone from the parade at Hastings.

DEC 1: Norman was in the battle for Walcheren.

DEC 16: we feel that the country is no longer in danger of invasion. Defences & obstacles are being removed.

1945

JAN 2: Telegram from the Under-Secretary of State for War- Norman reported missing Dec 28. The postmaster [Sedlescombe] telephoned to me at the District Council Offices [*to tell of the telegram*] out of kindness to save us a shock.

[*On 22 Jan the family learned that Norman had been taken prisoner*].

FEB 13: About 7.20 pm the house was shaken by an explosion. The war isn't over yet.

MAR 15: Men began repairing the damage done to our house by bombs.

APR 23: To-night the 'dim-out' ends for most places that are more than 5 miles from the coast. Hurrah! The Russians are well into Berlin.

MAY 2: Hitler's death is announced in Germany. Norman came home!

MAY 8: At three this afternoon by the wireless the Prime minister announced the surrender of Germany to the U.S. Great Britain & Russia. Whatlington Church was nearly full at a thanksgiving service at half past 7. Late, hearing bangs, we looked from a high window towards Battle & saw fireworks in front of the Abbey gateway.

MAY 13: To Battle by the 2.13 'bus from the Royal Oak for a service of thanksgiving on the Green. I went to the drill hall & marched with the casualty services. I wore my medal ribbons of the last war, the first time I think that I have done so.

JULY 21 [*Alan and Mary held a peace party at Hancox for the children of Whatlington*].

AUG 15: Surrender of Japan.
Two days holiday were proclaimed. About ten o'clock a bonfire was lit on the green at Whatlington. Norman was to have lit it had he been at home. [He had been ordered to re-join his regiment]. From the house we could see Battle Abbey gates lit by a fire on the green. Richard walked to Battle.

AUG 29: There was a procession at Battle celebrating victory. Hilary, Richard & Meriel went to it in the pony cart dressed in the style of about 100 years ago. Rose Smith [servant] lent Richard her father's old smock. They carried large trugs[1] full of fruit and vegetables. Benedicta Whistler dressed as a coster[2] drove a donkey cart. In the evening there was a torchlight procession for which Richard stayed.

---

1 Baskets
2 Fruit seller

NOV 17: Yesterday evening our windows were heavily shaken several times by explosions: probably sea mines were the cause.

DEC 31: This most memorable year leaves two great problems: how to ensure that atomic energy is not misused & how to convince all nations especially the greatest that complete national sovereignty must end & a world state be established; for if it is not, in some form or other, civilisation is under threat of destruction.

Mobile First Aid Unit
Back: only Miss Fuller, second from left, is known
Middle: far left Phyllis Hayden, unknown, unknown , Miss Bridger, Miss Haler, Mrs Connie Oliver, Mrs Sunnyside, unknown, unknown
Front from left: unknown, Mrs Crouch, unknown, Elspeth Blundell, Mrs Blain, Mrs Thomas

13 MAY 1945 THANKSGIVING SERVICE, BATTLE ABBEY GREEN

Quite a bit of detective work has been done to discover the date and origins of the photographs in this chapter, found in the Stan Elliott archive and in the family photo album of the Whistler family. We have concluded that three of them show the thanksgiving service in Battle on 13th May 1945 after Germany had surrendered; and one shows the celebrations on 29th August 1945, after Japan had surrendered. The main celebration on 13th May was a week after VE (Victory in Europe) Day, which among other things, gave thanks for the work in Battle during the war, of the voluntary services.

Address by the Dean of Battle 13 May 1945

In its 18th May 1945 issue, the *Sussex Advertiser* describes the event. The article carries no photo but the *Advertiser* description matches our photographs:

'Thanksgiving services were held throughout the district on Sunday for Victory in Europe, and from everywhere came reports of crowded churches and inspiring addresses. Parades of the various services also took place in nearly every town and village.

"It was to God we looked in those dark days during the past five years; in God we trusted because we were humbly confident that our cause could not be other than the cause of God. Now our confidence has been justified in a manner which can only be described as overwhelming."

These words were spoken by the Very Rev W W Youard, the Dean of Battle, at the town's victory thanksgiving service on the Green on Sunday.

Supported on a platform in front of the Abbey Gateway by the Rev A C Shrimpton (Curate), the Rev W C Soughton (Vicar of Netherfield), and a Methodist Minister the Rev H W Stewart of Hastings, the Dean was speaking to a parade of military and Home Front representatives and a large gathering of townspeople.

The parade, headed by the military contingent, included Home Guard, Army Cadet Force, members of the British Legion wearing their medals and headed by their standard bearers, the Police, NFS, Civil Defence Services with their flag, WVS, Scouts and Guides. They marched from the Green to the Watch Oak and back to the sounds of martial music from loudspeakers. The choir of the Parish church in scarlet cassocks and white surplices lined the front of the platform and led the singing of the hymns ' Now thank we all our God', 'All people that on Earth do dwell' and 'O God our help in ages past', which were accompanied on a harmonium.

"In May 1940", said the Dean, "Britain stood alone against the mightiest display of armed force the world had ever seen, with only her Navy, a gallant little Army just rescued from Dunkirk, and an Air Force splendid in quality but quite inadequate in numbers, to stand between her and destruction. The fate of the British Empire hung by a thread, but its faith and courage never for an instant faltered.

Then it was that there began a series of fatal mistakes on our enemy's part. But for those mistakes, humanly speaking, we could not have hoped to survive. Had God anything to do with those mistakes? Could we see His hand in them? These were questions beyond our ability to answer, but there was something to set us thinking hard in the words of the old hymn 'God moves in a mysterious way, His wonders to perform.'

"Here in Battle', continued the Dean, 'the war came very close to us at times. It was a strain on our nerves. Yet I think we are not sorry that we can claim to have been in the line of fire, to have shared peril with others. Our town lay on one of the routes of enemy aircraft, two of our fellow townsfolk lost their lives in a raid, while for more than two months the flying bombs brought danger so near that on some occasions our escape was little less than miraculous. Yet through all, we and our homes have been preserved, and we are alive today to say with full hearts: Thank God."

The Dean ended by remembering those – Battle men among them –

who had gone forth and would not return: "They were surely expecting, demanding, that the foundations of that better world looked forward to after 1918, should this time be so well and truly laid that upon them should rise an edifice full of strength and beauty and so permanent that it would last through the years. In Battle, two noble examples of buildings which had stood the test of the centuries: the Parish Church and the Abbey Gateway. The men who built them, built for the ages; they bent to the task all their energies, the best that was in them. Their whole heart and soul and mind went into the making. Might it be so in the building of the world of the future."

The *Sussex Advertiser* reports that there was also a Children's Day, presumably on the same day. The soldiers served tea for 300 and afterwards races were run.

The first photograph we have is from the Whistler family album:

Service of thanksgiving on the Abbey Green 13 May 1945

The Home Guard (stood down in December 1944 but not disbanded until 31st December 1945) are in front, the voluntary services behind them, and the platform out of picture to the right. Robert Emeleus is in the bottom right hand corner, flag in hand, next to his mother. Mrs Beaney is standing to the far left, by the pram. Everyone is looking to the right of picture, at the service being conducted, as described by the *Sussex Advertiser*.

Parade by voluntary services

The following are in the parade of voluntary services on their return from processing up to the Watch Oak (we know this is 13 May 1945 from Alan Moore's diaries):

Parade down Battle High Street

The tall man is Sir Alan Moore, Medical Officer of Health for Battle and District and behind him are volunteer nurses. In front of him is Miss Bridger. Wearing a Sergeant's stripes in the middle is Elspeth Blundell of the WVS, a local physiotherapist. The WVS usually wore dark green, but it's thought the light coats worn in this photograph must have been some kind of alternative uniform. Mrs Hewett of the Civil Defence, is walking out of shot; she and those behind her, were probably ambulance drivers, reminding us of the new roles many women undertook during the war, one of many lasting social consequences.

British Legion procession 13 May 1945

The following photo of the British legion matches the description of positioning in the *Sussex Advertiser* article about 13 May 1945 – a procession came from the Abbey as well as down the High Street. The clothes indicate this is in summer, not at a Remembrance Day service. The standard bearer in the lead is thought to have been Mr Frank Andrews.

British Legion procession, probably 13 May 1945

Celebrations of VJ Day: 13 August and 29 August 1945

There were two celebrations in Battle of VJ (Victory in Japan) Day (officially marked on 15th August): 13th August and 29th August. An account of the town's celebrations on 13th August 1945 is given in the *Hastings and St Leonards Observer* of 18th August 1945, with no photograph. The arrangements were made at the last minute by the British Legion and the NFS (National Fire Service). There was no open air service; there was bunting across the street and flags from residences, while crowds – not discouraged by early rain – swarmed along the High Street after breakfast. There was a service at St Mary's Church at 4.30 pm and a bonfire on the Abbey Green at 9.30 pm (lit by Mrs Arnould, local WVS Chief). Hornbrooks provided amplified music on the Abbey Green and at the Drill Hall where many people gathered; and the Battle Bonfire Boyes' fife and drum band played. People sang 'When the Lights Come on Again' – and they did, since the Council got the lampposts working again.

Probably 29th August 1945, celebrating the earlier VJ Day

The photo above comes from the Battle Museum of Local History archive. The entry just says 1945, parade by the Royal Naval Band. Judging from the dress, the event was in the summer, but the coach that is in the background of the British Legion photo, is not there, suggesting another event than the one on 13th May 1945, although the standards are present at the back of the crowd. We doubt this event was on 13th August 1945 when all the arrangements were last minute and there would probably not have been time to book the band.

That leaves the later 29th August 1945 VJ Day celebration, as the most likely date.

On Wednesday 29th August 1945, there was a fancy dress parade, decorated cars and bicycles, military and NFS displays, adult and children's sports and entertainments, dancing and a children's tea.

We do not know who took these photographs, but some of those who remember the Second World War in Battle, think that it is very likely to have been George Bramley, leader of Battle and Rural District Council at the time, and a very keen photographer.

BATTLE PEOPLE WHO DIED IN THE SECOND WORLD WAR 1939-45

This list follows the ones at St Mary's and the Memorial Hall, but we cannot exclude the possibility that further names may in due course come to light:

Civilians in Battle
Tom and Gladys Giles, Newsagents

Armed Services

Violet Edith Akehurst
A. Edward Barnes
John Ade Buckwell
Peter Cave
Cyril Donald Chatfield
William Cyril Crouch
Stephen Edward Dannreuther
Thomas Charles Fletcher
Reginald Arthur Edward Gamblen
William Clement Gander
John A. Hayes
Ronald Stanley Hills
Evan Griffith Hughes
William Deryck Kennard
Peter Anthony Lyle
Peter John Newbery
Charles David Noakes
Leslie Herbert Oliver
Lionel Harry Searle Rapley
Cyril Jack Robins
Charles Valentine Robins
Allan Cecil Sheather
Harry William Thorpe Sinden
J. Walter Skinner
Humphrey Rupert Cruse Soan
Albert Edward Spray
Philip Edward Stainton

The stories of those from Battle who died in the Second World War are told by George Kiloh in two articles, J4.1 WW2 Civilian Deaths in and from the Battle District and J4.2 Military Deaths from the Battle District 1939-45 on the Battle and District Historical Society's website www.battlehistory.btck.co.uk , in the Collectanea section.

Each story in the above list is a tragedy but that of **Violet Akehurst,** the only woman in the list, is unusual. She was the youngest woman to die in British and Commonwealth military service in the Second World War. Born at Robertsbridge on 23rd August 1925, by 1929 Violet Akehurst and her family had moved to Battle. She joined up as a Private in the ATS (Auxiliary Territorial Service) in August 1941 as soon as she was 16, and was posted to the 490th Heavy Anti-Aircraft Battery, Royal Artillery. This unit was famously deployed at Richmond Park, the mixed sex crews attracting large crowds and celebrity visits from Churchill and many others. We cannot be sure but it is possible that Violet was there. Churchill had controversial views about women pulling the trigger, but it turned out that they were very good, and probably better than the men, at setting the sights of the anti-aircraft guns. Violet contracted pneumococcal meningitis and at the specialist Bath Military Hospital she died on 24 November 1941. Violet was brought home to Battle and her military headstone (below) is in Battle Cemetery.

WORLD WAR TWO TIMELINE

1 September 1939	Hitler invades Poland
3 September 1939	Britain and France declare war on Germany
Early 1940	Rationing begins in Britain
10 May 1940	Churchill becomes Prime Minister
26 May-4 June 1940	British Expeditionary Force evacuated from Dunkirk
10 July-31 October 1940	Battle of Britain
7 September 1940-	The London Blitz
10 May 1941-22 June 1941	Operation Barbarossa – Hitler's invasion of Russia
27 November 1941	Allies take Tobruk in North Africa
September 1941	First extermination of prisoners at Auschwitz
7 December 1941	Japanese attack Pearl Harbour and USA enters the war four days later
January 1942-August 1945	Burma campaign
15 February 1942	Fall of Singapore
4-7 June 1942	Battle of Midway – decisive victory for Allies in the Pacific theatre of war
22 August 1942-2 February 1943	Battle of Stalingrad – Germany defeated
8–16 November 1942	Operation Torch – Anglo-American invasion of French North Africa
23 October 1942-11 November 1942	Battle of El-Alamein – Germany defeated

5 July 1943- 23 August 1943	Battle of Kursk – turned the tide to Russia on the eastern front
10 July 1943-17 August	Invasion by Allied troops of Sicily
8 September 1943	Italy surrenders but Germany takes over the battle
22 January 1944- 5 June 1944	Battle of Anzio
17 January 1944- 18 May 1944	Battle of Monte Cassino
27 January 1944	Siege of Leningrad (St Petersburg) lifted
June- Dec 1944	Significant Soviet offensive on eastern front
5 June 1944	Rome captured by the Allies
6 June 1944	D-Day: allied invasion of Europe
21 July 1944	Liberation of Guam
25 August 1944	Liberation of Paris
27 January 1945	Liberation of Auschwitz
4-11 February 1945	Yalta Conference of Churchill, Roosevelt and Stalin including arrangements for repatriation of Russian PoWs
12 April 1945	Franklin D Roosevelt dies, Harry S Truman becomes President of USA
16 April 1945	Battle for Berlin begins
30 April 1945	Hitler commits suicide
7 May 1945	Germany surrenders
26 July 1945	Clement Attlee becomes Prime Minister
6 August 1945	Bombing of Hiroshima
9 August 1945	Bombing of Nagasaki
14 August 1945	Japan surrenders

ACKNOWLEDGEMENTS AND SOURCES

Sources used (*underlined italics indicate websites*)

Angell, S: *Secret Sussex Resistance,* 1996

From BDHS Collectanea: (*http://battlehistory.btck.co.uk/Collectanea-OurVirtualLibrary/*)

Kiloh, G: *WW2 Civilian Deaths in and from the Battle*

Kiloh, G: *Military Deaths from the Battle District 1939-45*

Kiloh, G: and Clephane-Cameron, N *Battle at War*

http://www.battle-abbey.co.uk/

Battle Museum and YoubyYou Books: *Battle in Pictures,* 2006

Battle WI Scrapbook - Battle Museum

http://www.bbc.co.uk/history/ww2peopleswar/

Burgess, P and Saunders, *A Blitz over Sussex,* 1994

Elliott Archive, Battle Museum

ESWI book *East Sussex Within Living Memory,* 2006

Fraser, D: *Alanbrooke,* 1982

Hart- Davis, Duff: *Our Land at War,* 2015

https://www.eastsussex.gov.uk/leisureandtourism/localandfamilyhistory/localhistory/ww2/homefront

Hylton, Stuart: *Kent and Sussex 1940,* 2004

James, B A: *Moonless Night,* 2001

Kelly's Directory, 1939

Lampe, David: *The Last Ditch: Britain's Secret Resistance and the Nazi Invasion,* 2013

Lawrence, Andy 'The Impact of World War Two in Battle'. Undated essay from Stan Elliott archive

Mace, Martin F: *Sussex wartime relics and memorials,* 1997

http://www.massobs.org.uk/about/mass-observation-project

Middlebrook, M and Everitt, C: *Bomber Command War Diaries,* 1985

Minns, Raynes: *Bombers and Mash,* 1980

Nella Last's War, 2006

Parsons, M *Britain at War: Rationing*, 2000
Patten, Marguerite and Imperial War Museum *We'll Eat Again*, 1985
Pollard, R *A Pier without Peer: A History of Hastings Pier*
http://www.pillbox-study-group.org.uk/
Royal Air Force Museum incorporating Royal Air Force Historical Society https://www.rafmuseum.org.uk/about us/partners/raf-historical-society.aspx
Saunders, Andy 'The Battle of Britain and Battle' 2010 talk to the BDHS
Stacey, C P: *The Canadian Army 1939-1945 An Official Historical Summary*, 1948
Sussex Express and County Herald: *The War in East Sussex*, 1945
Taylor, A J P: *English History 1914-45*, 1965
Umfreville-Green, Brigadier General: *British Home Guard Pocket Book*
Wills , Henry: *Pillboxes: A Study of UK Defences*, 1940
Winslow, T E: *Forewarned is Forearmed*
https://www.womenslandarmy.co.uk/

Written histories

Written histories have been used, left behind by the following:
Cecil Bedwell, Ruth Chiverton, Stan Elliott, John Hill, Fred Holland, H S and M C Newbery, H G Seymour, Joan Thomas

Image acknowledgements

Every effort has been made to identify image ownership and seek permissions where practicable. We apologise for any omissions which will be acknowledged in any future editions.
Aircrew Remembered website, Simon Alexander, Battle and District Historical Society, Battle Museum of Local History, Bomber Command website, Carl Bellingrodt, Malcolm Cranfield, Kevin and Gina Doherty, Doullens town office, Elliott Archive, Adrian and Sarah Hall, Keith Harmer, Cherry Holmes, Michael Oliver, Ruth Pearson, Peter Seymour, Victoria Seymour, Mark and Ian Shore, Wikimedia Commons, Wikipedia, Whistler family, Women's Land Army.co.uk, WW2 Talk.
Chapter on John Shore: We are indebted to Ian and Mark Shore in preparing the material about their father; and to Mike Glazier and Peter Seymour for their advice. Several of the photographs in the chapter were sourced by Mark.

BATTLE MUSEUM OF LOCAL HISTORY

The Museum set in the Almonry Gardens

Battle Museum of Local History covers 125 million years of history with a wide range of exhibits from dinosaurs to primitive calculators, in almost 1000 objects. It contains the famous "Battle of Hastings axe" and has a permanent 1066 exhibition including special tapestries, films and a full size battle axe replica, in addition to a diorama showing the events of 14 October 1066.

The Museum is located in the Almonry Gardens at the north end of the High Street, having converted its current building in 2003 with the assistance of the Heritage Lottery Fund.

This independent Museum is a charity and is volunteer-run. It is active in the community, working in outreach and education with organisations such as Battle Town Council, Battle Library, Battle and Langton School, Battle and District Historical Society, and the Rotary Club of Battle. The Museum is accredited by the Arts Council England.

The Museum is open 10-4.30 Monday to Saturday from the start of April until the end of October. Entrance is free, donation appreciated. Friendly volunteers can advise visitors not only about the exhibits but also about what to see in Battle. Email: enquiries@battlemuseum.com or ring 01424 775955 during the season. See more at our website www.battlemuseum.com Facebook: enquiries@battlemuseum.com Twitter: @battlemuseum

The Battle and District Historical Society founded the Museum in 1956 and runs: monthly talks on a variety of historical topics; a research group and a reading group. Its website is: www.battlehistory.btck.co.uk The Collectanea section of the website contains over 100 articles about the local history of Battle and district.